# Daylight Saving Time

The Power of Growing Older

Previous Books

MEMOIR
*Walks with Sam*
*October Song*
*Any Road Will Take You There*
*There's a Hamster in the Dashboard*
*The Consequence of Stars*
*Accidental Lessons*

FICTION
*A Well-Respected Man*
*Things Behind the Sun*
*Rainbow Man*
*Night Radio*
*Sandman*

What people are saying about

# Daylight Saving Time

A remarkable read about one man's quest for happiness and fulfillment in the years he has left...an authentic and moving narrative with fittingly beautiful and powerful writing.
*International Review of Books*

With deeply woven, reflective writing, Berner takes cues from the events in his life, the seasons, and the natural world to craftily bundle a layered personal narrative that can only come from the power of growing older. Berner shows not only the meaning of his former years, but also the promise of those sure to come with the arrival of the first day of spring. *Daylight Saving Time* speaks wisdom from the heart.
**Nancy Chadwick**, author of *Under the Birch Tree: A Memoir of Discovering Connections and Finding Home*

*Daylight Saving Time* raises metaphysical and personal connections about the passing of time and the examined life. The author skillfully delves into both.
**Marc Frazier**, author of *Each Thing Touches*

A touching, introspective exploration of life as we age. Author David W. Berner offers his account of how he, in the wake of a heart attack, began to view life—a life we often take for granted—with a new and profound perspective. *Daylight Saving Time* is an exploration of what it means to truly live and grasp the beauty of life before it's gone.
**Ryan Lindner**, author of *The Half-Known Life: What Matters Most When You're Running Out of Time*

David's writing stimulates the mind and the heart, managing to mix the profound with everyday experiences, finding beauty in it all.
**Martin Wells**, author of *Lost for Words*

An engaging contemplation of the deeper issues in the midst of everyday life.
*Kirkus Reviews*

A philosophical inspection that captures the psyche of the aging soul ... adopting Proust-like attention to the details of pivot points, moments in time, and experiences unique to and representative of the 'season of light.'
**Diane Donovan,** *Midwest Book Review*

# Daylight Saving Time

## The Power of Growing Older

David W. Berner

BOOKS

London, UK
Washington, DC, USA

# CollectiveInk

First published by O-Books, 2024
O-Books is an imprint of Collective Ink Ltd.,
Unit 11, Shepperton House, 89 Shepperton Road, London, N1 3DF
office@collectiveinkbooks.com
www.collectiveinkbooks.com
www.o-books.com

For distributor details and how to order please visit the 'Ordering' section on our website.

Text copyright: David W. Berner 2023

ISBN: 978 1 80341 511 6
978 1 80341 520 8 (ebook)
Library of Congress Control Number: 2023933528

A CIP catalogue record for this book is available from the British Library.

Design: Lapiz Digital Services

UK: Printed and bound by CPI Group (UK) Ltd, Croydon, CR0 4YY
Printed in North America by CPI GPS partners

The author of this book does not dispense medical advice or prescribe the use of any technique as a form of treatment for physical, emotional, or medical problems without the advice of a physician, either directly or indirectly. The intent of the author is only to offer information of a general nature to help you in your quest for emotional and spiritual well-being. In the event you use any of the information in this book for yourself, which is your constitutional right, the author and the publisher assume no responsibility for your actions.

We operate a distinctive and ethical publishing philosophy in all areas of our business, from our global network of authors to production and worldwide distribution.

*For Dian Cécht, the Celtic god of healing*

*The years teach much which the days never know.*
—Ralph Waldo Emerson

# Author's Note

When I was a young man, it never occurred to me that anyone would grow old. Not my parents, my grandparents, and certainly not me. Time's passing is not a thought for the mind of the innocent. Still, reality catches up with you. Maybe it is when the first gray hair arrives, or when a knee buckles, or with the purchase of a pair of reading glasses, or when you ask the waitress to repeat the dessert choices for a third time, or when you realize how much you hate driving at night, or when the number of pills you take doubles, or when you start going to bed at sunset. Or maybe, more profoundly, when you have a heart attack at the age of 56, the same age as your father's nearly fatal attack.

With far fewer years in front than behind, I wonder about what it truly means to grow older. Don't we all wonder? We've never passed this way before. Maybe one should consider it an adventure.

When I began writing these words, the hope was to try to understand the journey, the unfolding of a life, to document it in the very moments that it was happening, piece by piece, day to day. To help see it, I chose a period of the year that some call the season of light, the space between the shifting of time, between Standard Time and Daylight Saving. It is a manmade phenomenon, yes, but it is also a remarkable period in the yearly ritual of preserving illumination, the darkest time on our calendars; yet we bravely stretch toward the equinox, toward something brighter, something beyond.

Like aging itself, what ended up on these pages are the small increments of a path that is nearly unnoticeable, so much coming in little surprises and unforeseen awakenings, frightening experiences, moments of celebration and resignation, sorrow, and delight, mixing like the chemicals of a mad scientist. And on a Sunday in late March, a week into a new spring, a wet and heavy snow began to fall, a leftover from a misplaced winter, a season not yet willing to let go.

# Prologue

Something was wrong. Still, I kept asking questions, taking notes. I was weak, sweating, my breathing labored. Desperate to sit down. But there was work to be done, a deadline, and so I kept at it.

There had been a shooting overnight in a residential neighborhood on Chicago's Northside, a part of town where crime of any kind was unusual, and I was talking to those who lived on the street where a man had been shot. My editor called. He wanted something on the story for the top-of-the-hour newscast on the radio station where I had been freelancing. After completing the interviews, I leaned against the outside of my car to write my report on my notepad and edit the recording. Heavy sweat rolled over my temples, and my chest began to cramp and tighten.

I sent the story to my editor and told him I needed to end my day. I was not well.

To drive myself home was my intention, but I could proceed only a few blocks at a time, pulling over to rest my head on the steering wheel. After a deep breath, one taken with alarming difficulty, I turned the car back on the road and knew then that I would not be going home.

In the hospital emergency room, two young doctors stood over me, both half my age. One with a clipboard, the other poking and prodding, listening to my chest through a stethoscope as I lay in bed.

"We think you're having a heart attack," he said, smiling. "But you came in at the right time. You're a poster child for what you're supposed to do."

Oddly, the news did not alarm me. Maybe it was the doctor's unexpected smile. Maybe I didn't fully understand. Maybe the reality of a heart attack made no sense. It should have. My father suffered one that nearly killed him when he was my age, exactly my age. Fifty-six. When he first had pain in his chest, he dismissed it as simple indigestion caused by eating a breakfast sweet roll too quickly. In hours, he was in an operating room, being prepped for bypass surgery. Someone has a heart attack in the United States every 40 seconds. He had been one of them. And now, I was one of them, too.

As nurses wheeled my bed down the hall to the room where doctors would insert a stent in my heart, I telephoned my then girlfriend, telling her where I was and what was about to happen. I asked her not to worry and to call my sons. Let people know. I wanted them to know.

The surgeon asked if I wanted to watch.

"I can do that?" I asked.

Through the groin, a probe was inserted and snaked through my upper leg to my chest to my heart. On the equipment's monitor I could see the gray shadow of my pumping muscle and the surgeon's instrument.

"In a moment, you're going to feel a lot better," he said.

With uncanny precision, he cleared the plaque and inserted the stent. I could see it happening, all in shades of gray, as if watching one of the early video games that you played from a primitive black-and-white electronic console.

"How's that feel?" he asked.

Transformed and still alive.

Heart attacks are America's number-one killer. They happen when blood flow to the heart is suddenly blocked, the heart is denied oxygen, and if not treated quickly, the heart muscle begins to die. With immediate treatment, you may be able to prevent or limit the damage. Most people who have one survive. I was lucky. No damage. I was given no restrictions. Just a few weeks of rest. But what had happened that day would stay with me for a long time.

About a month after surgery, during a follow-up with the doctor, I told him I had been out on my bike.

"Is it bad that I rode 12 miles the other day?" I asked.

"You did *what*?"

Maybe a little early to do that, he said, hesitating slightly, seemingly to be sure he was addressing my question in a measured tone. But I felt fine, I told him. Just be careful, he said.

Living was what I was determined to do. Holding on tight to the years that remained was everything. Some would see the heart attack as a wake-up call, a reminder of the human will. And it was, and it is for many who struggle moving on after a health scare. I didn't initially find myself in that category. Instead, I carried on a bit too bravely, unknowingly attempting to ignore the fragility of life. What I needed more was psychological healing, the awakening to the clarity of life's most precious purpose. I was detecting more lines on my face. More gray in the remaining hair. I would now be taking more medication. But I keep climbing the mountain, believing the view must get better with each step. *What do you do with what you see from way up here? Do you simply take a photograph, or do you dive into the horizon with everything you've got?*

I didn't think there was any real choice.

# 1

I awake dreaming, unable to sleep. The time change has shifted my rhythms, body, and mind. It may have been the late night and the cocktails at Clinton Street Social Club. Something made with rye whiskey. My digital watch reads 5:30 a.m. but I am unsure if what it displays is the old or the new time, if the hour on my watch has shifted on its own.

My wife sleeps at my side in the downstairs bedroom of her daughter's place. It is a good home in Iowa City, not far from the football stadium, a short drive to the downtown, a half-mile easy walk to the Sidekick coffee shop, a new place that is said to be lined with ceiling-high bookcases. Discovering new coffee shops is a hobby, of sorts. *I could go now. Are they open early on a Sunday?* Instead, I use the bathroom and return to bed and stare into the dark. Book titles bounce in my head. It's in the mist of my mind, something about aging, about time. Something on how one reckons with change, the inescapable turn of the earth and sun that none of us escape. Not that we would necessarily want to, not that anyone wants to, yet we are designed, it seems, to fight against it in small and big ways.

Some exercise might shake me into balance, a practice I've tried to stay with, albeit sporadically, since the heart attack several years ago. So, I step to the next room and do 20 pushups. They've come easier since I started this routine two weeks ago. Nine was hard last week. Now, I'm performing more than double this. I squat into a chair and stand, and do it again, over, and over. Twenty-five. I try to touch my toes but can't. Still, I pull forward to the ground and feel the muscles awaken. The body resists but I battle back. I can't find anything sturdy enough to wrap an exercise band around. A door doesn't shut tight enough to hold the strain. I use the leg of the long TV stand

and sit on the floor, twist the band around it twice and begin, snapping the band toward my chest. It is not tight enough for the best resistance, so I do more than my usual 20, over and over, with tightness in my chest, stomach, arms, and the middle of my back until I am out of breath.

"Good morning," Leslie whispers.

In the murky light, we hold each other for more than a minute, saying nothing.

"Are you going soon?" She asks this as others in the house, including the dog, are still sleeping.

"I am."

"What time is it?"

"I think it's a little after six, but I'm not sure."

"You should go."

I want to read first, Patti Smith's *M Train*, and recline on the oversized couch and turn on the book light attached to the back cover. Smith writes in small bites but with a keen sense of observation and heightened awareness of the singular moment. Self-awareness discovered right in front of you. I finish one chapter, only a few pages.

The titles of books unwritten, of jacket cover descriptions, come again to me. *But who would read it?*

I now remember the dream. I'm with two people I do not know, and we sit at a long table. My phone is in the center and a former publisher of two of my books is on the other end by the phone's speaker. It is a negotiation at some level, and no one is happy. There is no argument, but instead there is disrespect; tension fills the room, something ugly in the unspoken. Another dream is recalled. It is a worry dream. In the real world, my younger son and his wife drove to Milwaukee last night from their home outside Chicago to see a concert. Part of this true story is the dream—reality and fantasy mixing. In the dream, my heart beats with unease as I wait for a phone call from a police officer, a call from an emergency room doctor, a call that never comes.

From the window, I see hints of the sun struggling with the clouds, and there is no wind, as the trees are still. I throw water on my face, pull on my wool cap, and layer up for the chill. There is no notebook with me on this trip. Writing longhand at the coffee shop—a slower, reflective process—might do me good this morning. *Maybe the shop sells little Moleskines. Do I have a pen?* With my laptop and Patti's book under my arm, I walk along Melrose Street, a slight uphill climb past small homes that appear to be stuck in the 1970s. There are few cars, fewer people. A man rides his bicycle, bundled in a heavy coat and ski mask.

The coffee shop is at the end of a new modern complex of offices and condos. The sign nearby calls it luxury living, far different than the homes nearby. The café is sleek, clean, and neat. As advertised, books line two walls, floor to ceiling. The shelves are labeled with large, handcrafted signs—Nonfiction, Young Adult, Animals, Fiction. There are emerald-colored sofas facing each other, and a modern coffee table sits between them; a fancy new version of checkers is in the center. A long line of black tables and chairs is across from the counter a few feet away, and to the right, a play area for kids with a wooden toy train and more chairs. I like coffee shops without play areas, preferring the tattered and worn, exactly what this café is not. The concept of the place, I had been told, is to build a community for readers and thinkers, and yes, families and children, too. There is no WiFi.

A young woman is alone with her laptop at a small table at the far end of the shop. Another is behind the counter, and to the right, near the children's area, is an older woman with a spray bottle and a hand rag. She cleans the toys that have been left scattered on a large play table.

"Good morning," she says.

"It is a good morning, isn't it?"

I'm not sure why I say that.

I order a latte and pay, and while waiting, I browse the books. Two volumes of *The Best Time We Ever Had* are at eye level, Claire Lombardo's big book of family. I interviewed her before a small crowd at the Hemingway Birthplace Home in Oak Park not long ago when the book was first released. She is an Iowa Writers' Workshop graduate. They are proud of her here.

"Where do you get your books?" I ask the older woman as she continues to clean.

"She gets them from bookstores and online."

I had thought maybe they had been donated.

"I'm a writer," I say.

This seems such a pretentious, silly statement. Anyone, many say, can be a writer these days with some time and money.

"I'm visiting family in town. I'm from Chicago."

"What do you write?"

There's the book coming out next year, the one about walking my dog and the history of the literary walker. I tell her, too, about my fiction, a little about the memoirs. But I cut myself off. I don't like the way I sound, talking about myself.

"What's your name?"

I tell her. But leave out the W, the middle initial. I use it because there's another David Berner out there. I don't know why I delete this from our conversation. The writer in me carries the W with purpose. The other part of me does not.

"Okay. Well, she might be popping in later," she says, referring again, I assume, to the shop's owner.

"I'll be here for a little bit."

I don't expect to meet her.

Light is now rushing through the large windows. The morning has fully arrived, despite the manmade recalculation of time. And at my small table, the tiniest one in the shop,

I find on my phone the notes made earlier this morning—ones I regrettably could not write in my forgotten notebook—open my laptop and lift the coffee to my lips. There are two hours to read and write before a big breakfast with the family. On the café's speaker system "Blue Velvet" is playing—Bobby Vinton's version, the number-one hit from sometime in the early 1960s. The Bobby Vinton from my hometown, Pittsburgh, the town I left decades ago. The song is a sad one of lost love and longing, of time misplaced, of regret and wounds that won't heal. So many people have cried to that song, sitting alone, and wondering *what if*, and considering those who have moved on, believing all heartache can be healed with time. Time—that great healer. Time—that thief of our most precious moments. Time—the only thing in the end that truly proves what matters.

Today, on this early November morning, everyone in Iowa has had one more hour added to their experience, more time for living, a chance to recover 60 minutes. It is Standard Time now, and everywhere in homes and apartments all around me the clocks are being adjusted to reflect a new reality, a manmade illusion. So, with this new hour all mine, I read, drink this good coffee, and write, and before long I walk the busier street back to the house as the world awakens and there are so many places to go.

# 2

This is the city of Algren, the city of Sandburg's shoulders. Hemingway lived in a Northside apartment in this town for a time. It was a brick row house on Dearborn Street. I hope to see it again sometime, stand in front of it. Sherwood Anderson lived in a boardinghouse in Chicago, becoming a writer only after suffering a nervous breakdown and abandoning his business career. I walk on the gray streets of these men, this city, wearing a favorite coat, an old olive-green barn jacket. If I could wrap myself in this garment every day—in July humidity or February freeze—I would be content.

Before awakening, I had dreamt of my sister, the anniversary of her birthday two days before. In a few weeks, I will be 63. She would have been 57.

When Diane comes in my sleep, she is always laughing. The laugh is all I have. I own nothing of hers. No clothing. No favorite coffee mug. Not the stainless-steel lighter she carried. Her ashes are stashed under my nightstand, what remains of them after scattering handfuls of dust at the bottom of mountains where she skied and had hoped to ski, and inside Heinz Field, the home of her beloved Steelers. I also have little of my dead mother or father. There is Mom's wedding ring, and her Dickens-esque Christmas carolers—the ones crafted at a ceramics class when I was a boy. I have her prized recipes, a binder of words and photos she constructed for me as a gift when I moved to my first apartment after college. There's Dad's charcoal drawing of a Great Dane, framed and resting on a bookshelf. I have his wallet and an old worthless Timex watch. I wear his onyx ring. Still, much is missing, most significantly and strangely, the dates of each of their deaths. The anniversary of my sister's birthday is November 2nd, and I

forever acknowledge the birthdays of my father and mother—
May 17th and August 1st—but the calendar days marking their
deaths have been lost, continually forgotten. It was early in
December for my mother, and it was February, I believe, for
my father. *Wasn't it summertime for my sister?* I am not sure of
any of it. The exact dates, I have learned to reject.

Earlier this morning, before heading to the city, I carried my
notebook and a book to the shed behind the house where I write.
I scribbled some notes and random thoughts in the quiet, words
about my sister. My old guitar, the nicked and beaten Yamaha,
leaned against the east wall and I found myself drawn to it. Two
different chord progressions had been knocking around in my
brain for a few days. I ran through both and found something
new in each one, a tempo and a phrasing in the nonsense lyrics.
*I must remember this.* I find myself forgetting more often than not
these days.

When I returned to the house, my wife was awake.

"I think I need to go west," I said, drinking coffee at the
kitchen counter.

"I have always been pulled west. You know that about me."

"New Mexico. Wide open spaces. I think that's it."

She smiled.

On the train to the city, my notebook on my lap, I continued
the earlier stream of thoughts, writing fragments, drawing stars
with my pen next to the words I wanted to recall. I wrote a
haiku, a Monday ritual:

the vanishing hour
brittle brown under my boots
the season of sleep

The train wailed as it made its frequent stops. There was a man
on his computer filling in the blanks of a spreadsheet; a woman

chattering through her Bluetooth earpiece, something about a difficult client; a young man with an oversized backpack sleeping with his head against the window, and another reading the news on his phone, maybe a story about another Trump tweet in an upside-down world.

Now, here I am, walking from Union Station. There is a bite in the air, but the sun is bright. I stop in a grassy, tree-shaded corner on the campus of an office complex next to one of the world's tallest buildings to take a phone photo of my boots on fallen leaves, a companion to the haiku. All around me, there is an unforgiving rush. If one were to stop walking, the conveyor could malfunction, and bodies would tumble. No time for anything but to match the pulse, and so I step up to the city's demands, an attempt to beat the ticking clock, the mechanism that mocks the sun. In this contemporary world, we no longer look to the heavens for guidance, for there are other means to mark our days in a modern life.

At the coffee shop with the high windows and the stone front where I plan to write for a few hours before walking the three blocks to my college office, I order a black coffee in a ceramic mug, and unpack my notebook and laptop from my bag. In an interior pocket there is a tattered paperback of Rilke's *Letters to a Young Poet*. I came to this book late in life, not as a young man and certainly not as a poet, but instead as someone in his forties who had been searching, the way a poet might. For years, I had hoped that carrying Rilke's words near would somehow help me understand what has always rumbled in my gut, a burning inside that sometimes unnerves me, but also keeps me alive. Twenty years later, Rilke's book with its faded dog-eared pages remains within reach, and I am still searching, no longer to discover but instead to mark the path of the years. And now, from my chair in the café and through the big window, I see the many faces passing by—the faces of men and women chasing life. A light snow begins to fall, and in an instant, I no longer wonder what has been, or what is to come, but wish instead to understand only what is.

# 3

4:10 a.m. I am rested. Not sleepy. Still, it is far too early for much of anything. I remain under a single sheet, trying to find the coolest part of the pillow to rest my head and to maneuver with ease so as to not disturb my wife. I had awakened earlier to use the bathroom, found the house too warm, and adjusted the thermostat. Too cold for her, I'm sure. I sleep better in the chill; she may not.

Staring into the dark, my head is jumbled with random, fleeting thoughts.

The day before at the college, one of my students had asked my advice about her remaining classes, what to choose as she approached graduation, the class she wanted to take or the easier one.

"The Beat Literature class or yoga?"

I weighed out the options.

"With other rigorous senior classes, easy might be better," I suggested. "Plus, you're the kind of person who will end up reading those books even if you don't take the class."

In my undergrad days, the Beats were unknown to me, and yoga was a foreign concept from a faraway land. Home was a steel town of deer hunters and football players. Adventure and the idea of enlightenment only came my way in time, the kind of enlightenment I didn't know I needed. I wonder now: *Have I lived the life I have wanted to live? Am I living it now? And how in heaven did I get here?* I think of New Mexico, and of the house in my neighborhood I had noticed the evening before that had been fully decorated for Christmas, nearly two months before the holiday, bright red and white lights illuminating a giant tree, outlining the house, and the front door. No sign of Jesus, though Halloween pumpkins decayed on the front porch. *Why are we in a hurry?* I think of my birthday, two weeks away. The other day I noticed how fatigue comes easier, not a physical tiredness or out-of-breath weariness, but the heaviness of some ancient timepiece. My father died in his seventies. So did my mother. My sister succumbed to alcohol in her fifties. My aunt, my mother's younger sister, is in her eighties. *Does she still smoke? I should call my aunt.*

With my mind still flittering, I slip from the covers, step out of bed, and pet the sleeping dog at my feet. At the kitchen counter, I write in my notebook—about the student, about my aunt, New Mexico, about my age. There was a need to look up the day's horoscope on my phone. Not something I often do, but do it anyway. The personality trait on one website suggests vindictiveness and a lack of self-confidence. No doubt I've been there. Not proud when those elements of my humanity appear in broad daylight. Another site says I can be emotional, creative. I'll take that. Also listed are the famous who share my birthdate. Voltaire was born on November 21, 1694. He was imprisoned in the Bastille for his writings mocking French royalty; his most famous works were banned for his criticism of religion and the justice system. He never married, never had children, he had a famous love of coffee, and in his old age set up a successful watchmaking business. Catherine the Great and King Louis XV wore his watches. There's a legend that Voltaire wore one of his own timepieces on his deathbed as leaders of the Catholic Church visited, hoping to persuade him to retract his condemnations and confess to his sins. Voltaire refused. He was denied a Christian burial. Certainly, as time ran out, right there on his own watch, Voltaire knew he had lived the life he had wanted to live.

I return to bed to find sleep again.

Two hours pass. I make coffee and smear avocado on grainy toast. At the kitchen counter, I scan emails and respond to students in need of authorizations for spring semester classes, agree to a flyer for an event about memoir writing at Chicago's Harold Washington Library that I have been asked to moderate, and remind my teaching colleagues to donate a few of their authored books to a student conference on campus. I text my son just to say hello and then take the stairs to the basement. With music playing from the speakers—Amos Lee, Bob Dylan, and Band of Horses—I do 25 squats and 20 pushups and pull on the exercise band 30 times in various positions. I have awakened and am breathing heavier. Afterward, I make more coffee and return to the kitchen counter. *New Mexico*. I search websites for casitas to rent come late spring, adobe homes in the high desert. My wife is awake now and comes to the dining table.

"I just want you to know. I'm searching for places."

"I'm okay with that. Will there be rattlers?"

"They won't hurt you if don't provoke them."

"Still. I want to know what to do."

There are no such creatures in the prairie grasses outside Chicago.

"Temperatures should be in the 50s and 60s at that time of year," I say.

"Do we fly into Albuquerque?"

"Yes. There's one property in the mountains south of Santa Fe. I like it."

Just as I say this, my train of thought is broken by music from the basement, a song on the playlist I had allowed to continue—The Beatles' "In My Life."

"You know I want this at my memorial when I'm dead, right?"

"I've lost track," my wife says. "You keep adding and then changing. You need to write this down."

"This and The Velvet Underground," I half-joke.

"Let's have a death weekend. We can document all the wishes. Who's being cremated? Big or small memorials, or not? What songs?"

"Death weekend?"

"Yep, Death Weekend."

I stand to refill my coffee, feeling secure in the knowledge that whatever is decided on Death Weekend won't be needed or executed anytime soon. Then, I make a mental note to revisit an old favorite, Allen Ginsberg's last poetry book, *Wait Till I'm Dead*, and promise myself again to call my aunt.

# 4

The track stretches east and west until it disappears. In the haze I see the train's single headlight, growing in size as it moves closer. Soon, the chug and clank are unmistakable, the sound growing like the headlight, its size determined instead by decibels. It is such a powerful animal, the train, tons of unstoppable steel. Slowing it down takes an army. Stopping it takes a mile. The lapels of my barn jacket are up around my neck. The rush of the train's force takes my breath away. Forty miles per hour doesn't seem so fast when driving a car, but here before the power of millions of pounds, it is unnerving.

Graffiti is scrawled on the freight cars. Not one or two cars, but every one that passes, words and symbols moving too quickly to read or decode. Some are gang symbols, no doubt. Tagging of some kind. Some are names, painted in purple and blue and red. Some 4 feet tall, written in cartoonish lettering. *Chad. Nicky.* There's one in orange that reads *God is Good*. It is art from the margins, the words of the prophets, like the lyrics of the Simon and Garfunkel song.

I telephoned my aunt last night and delighted in her forever-girlish laugh. At 82 years old, she has the heart of a young woman. Still crazy, always have been, she said, giggling. I asked the questions one would expect after not talking to her for nearly a year. She did, too. But the call was not to gain knowledge; it was certain each of us was still there, 500 miles apart, our hearts still beating, our lives being lived, our trains still running. I think of her and that call as I board the ride to the city, climbing the train car's steps behind an old woman who struggles in her ascent. I wait, a bit impatient, and hate myself for it. So, I take a breath and ask if the woman might need a hand. She smiles and shakes her head. Her eyes are gray and watery. Her silver hair is tight under a stylish black hat, the strands tumbling out at the temples, and a heavy long-strapped leather carryall in her hand. I wonder if my aunt has ever been on a train such as this, the woman who outlived my parents by a decade, the woman who had a falling out with my mother—her older sister—and found the strength to repair what was left in the final months when my mother was dying in a nursing home, the woman who lives alone in her own apartment, who still loves a good gin and tonic, who cherishes what remains of her independence, the woman I have not seen in a long time and may never see again.

Train commuters sit alone, one to each of the double seats. A girl with magenta-dyed hair sits two seats in front of me; another young woman applies blush before a small mirror in a forward-facing seat. I'm finishing Patti Smith's book, the final pages. With all the seats taken but one, a woman claims her spot next to me. She is my age, I'm guessing. Immediately she is busy, adjusting her bag, removing her gloves, and placing a thick document in her lap. There is an air of determination and borrowed time. I move closer to the window to allow her more room. She appears to need it, and hurriedly flips through the pages of the document, scribbling, if not on every page, then on every other one. Her energy takes space, filling a sizable portion of the immediate world. Some people can do that. Some by who they are, some by what they do. It is not always welcome. The car is silent except for the cranking of the train's wheels and the slap of the turning pages of what now has the unbroken attention of a woman on a mission. This has me thinking about missions, those assignments we give ourselves: Secure a good job, have children, be an artist, become a yoga master, learn to play the piano. My mother always wanted to write a book but didn't have the slightest idea of how to begin. My father had the hands and heart of an artist, his sketches and drawings aroused awe, but he became an insurance agent instead. My sister's mission was to tame her demons. She never did.

Before bed last evening, I was in the garden using the flashlight on my phone to recover the remaining sage plants before the predicted hard freeze. My wife had used some of the herb for our dinner of squash ravioli and it triggered the ancient love of earthy perfume. It was in the northern Arizona desert that I fell in love with sage, the wild plants hugging the rocks and dusty ground. When I plucked a grayish-green leaf, the sweetness of its scent filled me. The plants were in the west corner of the small garden space, two large ones, not dense but rather tall. I snapped the barky branches close to the ground and gathered them in my hand like a bunch of flowers. At the kitchen counter, I pulled away the leaves from the branches. *This is a lot of sage*, I thought, so much of the plant Charlemagne had cultivated in monastery gardens, the plant Greek physician Dioscorides claimed prevented disease, English botanist John Gerard believed was good for the brain, and Native Americans insist is sacred. I recalled a lotion I acquired in Santa Fe many years ago made with the oil of sage. I put the leaves from the garden in a plastic bag and placed them on a shelf in the refrigerator. A Google search turned up a recipe for sage lotion. I ordered beeswax pellets. Coconut and grape seed oil were in a kitchen cupboard, ingredients needed for a recipe for shifting one's mood.

I'm in the city now and the African American man standing bent on his wooden cane and his ragged coat around his back shakes his cup of coins just a few feet outside the doors of Union Station's Jackson Street entrance where concrete meets the river.

"God bless you," he says, and wishes me a good day.

I smile but do not offer a gift. Not today. As I walk beyond him, he repeats his words, ones he must deliver in repetition, like prayers in confession, every few minutes in every hour of his day. What brings him here to this place? What is his mission? What was it then? What is it now? Is time on his side? Walking just in front of me is another man, maybe in his late sixties, protected in a long expensive wool coat. He too carries a cane, one with a brass tip and an elegantly carved handle. He wears a blue baseball-style cap with a Ralph Lauren horse on the brim, and he carries a leather bag strapped over his chest and shoulder. Affluent he is, yet he is beaten. His walk is crooked and labored; he leans to one side, favoring the other. His feet, guarded in shiny leather, plod forward in opposite directions, the right fighting the left. In his mind he is certain of his target, his destination, I have witnessed, and still, he is unsure, it seems, of his purpose. What does he think as he trudges along? Age does not discriminate.

Many hours later, after the day is done and I am on my way to the train station for the ride home, the change in light produced by the seasonally altered clock is evident. It is not dark, but it's getting there, and lights in the shops and businesses along the street appear like guiding lanterns, lamps on a medieval road. At the bridge near the river a few dozen feet from where the old Black man had stood this morning with his cup of coins, I notice words scrawled in white on the rust-colored metal abutment under the walkway of the bridge: *All is Holy*—words of the prophets, the ones written on the subway walls and tenement halls, like the words seen this morning on all those trains, or the "God bless you" offered to me by the voice of a beggar. Reaching the other side of the bridge, I look for him, that old man, but he is gone. He has, I hope, found some momentary peace, the kind sage might offer, and some warm place to rest to watch the shrinking light and the emerging night swallow another day.

# 5

Snow is forecast. It is to be an early arrival for the coming storm. Cold and snow so soon in November seems like a punishment. In a day, the young man who gathers and mulches away the thousands of autumn leaves in our yard will arrive with his big riding machine. This puts me on a ladder next to the garage gutter, removing the accumulated small branches and dead leaves that have left the maples and the magnolia. I'm using a hand leaf-blower, holding it awkwardly while bracing myself on the top step of the ladder. It's a necessary job, and I hope to force as many leaves to the ground as possible for the big machine to take them away. And then tomorrow, when the yard is clear of autumn's debris, I'll walk the spreader around and toss winter fertilizer over the grass. It's an exercise in hope— hope the spring will come as scheduled, hope the nutrients will do their work, hope our tired old lawn will strengthen and thrive even though the grass roots are older than I am.

My phone vibrates in my pocket. I don't hear it ring, as the blower is too loud. I finish a section of the gutter and step down and find a text from my son. It's a photo of one of the brackets of a handrail that has lost one of three screws, and the words: *help me with this*. After a few texts back and forth to clarify, it seems one screw has stripped from the drywall and will no longer hold. *I know what you need*, I text. *Put the screw in the palm of your hand and send a pic*. We agree I will look when I come to his house tomorrow to watch football. Both of my boys grew up Steeler fans even though they lived outside Chicago. The Pennsylvania-born father has had some influence.

The following morning, I'm at the hardware store. The dog has come along. The owners don't mind a leashed pet and she is as familiar with them as they are with her. She receives a couple of hellos, and at least one healthy and vigorous petting from one of the regulars as I work through an array of small screws and wall anchors along the stretch of one long aisle. Flatheads, Phillips heads, brass and steel, galvanized and even hard plastic ones. I gather a handful of varied sizes, pay at the counter where the dog gets another petting and a rub around the ears, return to the house to get my toolbox, and head north to my son's.

*35 minutes—on my way*, I text.

With the screws in a small brown paper bag and a toolbox of screwdrivers, wrenches, a tape measure, and a hammer resting on the passenger seat, I think to myself, *I am my father. This is what he did.* When I got married and moved to Chicago, my father and mother visited often, and when they did, Dad would arrive at the door after the seven-hour drive with his toolkit in hand. He repaired a wall socket, fixed the loose leg of a kitchen chair, re-secured the dryer vent on the outside of the house, and one weekend in the summer, built an entire deck off the kitchen door. There was the wooden play gym with the swing and the slide. And I am certain, that sometime during those Mr. Fix-It days, my father repaired a handrail or two.

Weeks before, I had been at my son's, helping with some yard work and the rearrangement of his downspouts to avoid water seepage in the basement.

"Dad, you don't have to do all this," my son said.

"But I'm here. I can cut the hedges in the back if your electric trimmer is working."

"I don't want you to spend all your time with me doing things."

"I don't mind," I say. "Honestly, I don't."

My son put his arm on my shoulder.

"Dad," he said, "I got this."

In the remaining hours of that afternoon, we put down our tools and my son showed me the blocks of exotic wood he had purchased to turn on his lathe, we traveled together to the woodworking store so he could check out the newest gadgets, and grabbed lunch at a taco place he had heard was amazing.

It's a few minutes before kickoff when I arrive. My son points to the handrail.

"I'm going to take this off the wall and I want you to watch so you know how to do this," I say.

My son nods.

Holding one of the anchors in my hand, I model how to line it up with the hole in the wall and tap it in place with a hammer. The rail is replaced, one screw at a time, slowly turning the final one in the newly anchored hole.

"I've seen those before," he says, referring to the anchor. "Maybe used them when hanging a picture on the wall?"

"Yeah. I think I got this next time it happens."

We watch the game, eating crackers and cheese, homemade guacamole, and chips. Hours later, after the sun has fallen from the sky, I drive home in the November night. And as I turn to the highway toward home, a single snowflake hits my windshield and quickly melts. Another lands; another one disappears, another and another. It is the snow that had been in the forecast, yet I am surprised at its arrival. A snowflake, in order to form, needs ice crystals from the sky and dust particles from the air and ground. You might say a snowflake is half heaven and half earth, each a separate entity until clinging together to create the oneness of snow. The radio announcer suggests that millions of these flakes will cling together overnight to give us an inch or two on the ground by morning, enough to blanket us and change the landscape. But, the radio says, in days ahead, a warming trend will return and melt it all away.

# 6

I am on one of the first express trains, two hours after sunrise, an earlier event in these Standard Time days. The sunlight comes sooner now; the dark comes faster, too. The sun is welcome—the muted grace of its rays through the blinds—but the early emergence of night brings with it a disquieting melancholy. Talk of doing away with the seasonal time change has been going on for years at the state capitol, but on my phone's newsfeed this morning is evidence that its days, or more specifically its hours, may be nearing an end. The Illinois Senate had passed a plan to do away with Standard Time and make Daylight Saving Time permanent. The idea came out of a high-school classroom project. Students were assigned to address something they wanted to change or alter and then create a campaign to see it through. Now, it is reality and moving through the legislature.

I look at my wristwatch. 8:46 a.m. It would be 9:46 a.m. under Daylight Saving. *Where does that hour go?* Time is a manmade concept, so man can alter it at will. He has, of course, with the clocks in autumn and spring. We are told time is a dimension. The Bible believes in a clear beginning and end. Zen teachings suggest time is an illusion, and only a series of tiny separate instants, like movie frames. Native Americans once relied entirely on the movement of the sun to measure their days and lives. Still, no matter our calculations, time is passing without pause. No way to slow it down. That missing hour is still there. It is only reimagined. We measure time with clocks and calendars, even train schedules, but we cannot say or understand what truly happens when time passes.

The mid-November weather brings a brisk and frigid wind. Gray skies match the color of the Chicago River. I make a fast track over the bridge and into the heart of the city, my watch cap pulled down over my ears, my scarf protecting my neck and nearly covering my mouth and cheeks. If I were relying on the weather to measure time, this autumn morning would be a day in late January. I pass workers in the street who are waist-high in a long hole in the concrete, laying steel pipe. *How do they work in this? Eight hours a day. Long stretches in this weather either damage a man or strengthen him.* Another man bundled in a down coat, ski mask, and thick boots stands at the entrance to a parking garage, waving an orange flag. It's his job to entice drivers to choose his place to house their cars for the day. *What a terrible job on a morning like this.* At the corner two blocks from the coffee shop, as I stand, shielding myself from the wind and waiting for the pedestrian traffic light to change and a line of cars to pass, a young man in a short jacket and a Cubs baseball cap approaches from behind.

"Do you know what time it is?" he asks.

*Is he really asking me this, this question that appears to be on cue, as if reading my mind?* I adjust the bag on my shoulder and lift the sleeve of my coat to see my wristwatch.

"9:14," I say.

"And is the Red Line this way?" he asks, pointing east.

"State Street. It's the subway. Go down the steps."

As he nods and strides off, it occurs to me again how odd it was for him to ask for the time. Does he not have a phone? Did he not see the big digital clock on the bank sign across the street? And what is it that he is attempting to calculate?

The next morning, I'm in the shed with plans to write. Across the lawn on the other side of the street, there are carpenters balancing themselves on high framing. I cannot see them, but I hear their hammers striking nails and the murmur of their voices, men and women working together to beat the coming days of dwindling light and cold, hoping to complete the outside work on a new home before retreating inside. It's a race. Time is chasing them. I'm here to write, but instead a memory of my father arrives from long ago to remind me—he was once one of those men, shuffling 2x4s and driving 16-penny nails through pine under summer's sun and in winter's bitter air. He was once a young man, only 17, who had dropped out of high school to work after his father left. His entire life was in front of him, yet full of uncertainties. Still, pounding nails—straight and clean into soft wood—and breathing in the fragrance of sawdust after a fresh cut was his salvation, his hands building something that gave him control over his creation. Those were tough days, but good ones, shaping his world in the belief that creating something that stood the test of time was the mark of a man. Those homes he helped build in the South Hills of Pittsburgh are still standing. Families live in them. Children sleep at night in the bedrooms he framed.

I am ashamed, thinking again about my inability or my hard reluctance to recall the days of my parents' deaths. Why this is so, I'm certain, is far more complicated than I know. It's not so simple, making peace with ghosts. And why is it on this morning, with the sound of carpenter's work echoing around me, that I find myself again wondering?

I google my father's name, and the search turns up my mother's obituary in the online version of the *Pittsburgh Post-Gazette*. It was December 1, 2011. She was 77. I remember how cold the evening was. I held her hand at her bedside. I don't believe she knew I was there.

I find my sister's obit. July 8, 2016. She was 53. There was a phone call from the emergency room in the early morning hours. She had destroyed her liver and there was nothing more that could have been done.

I rest my back against the chair, adjust the space heater, and stare between the window blinds at earthy shades of brown and white, bare trees and snow. I sit like this for a few minutes. I hear my breath. When I return to the computer, it takes three different search engines to discover my father's death notice, but I eventually discover his obituary at a site named Legacy.com. Not sure why it is there and nowhere else. That night quickly comes back to me. My father hanging on in his deathbed on the second floor of my parents' home, where he had been for many days. I was sitting in the living room with my mother when his heart stopped. The website says he died on February 28, 2004. He was 71. Nine years older than I am today.

A candle burns on the desk but offers no shadows, not in the cloudy light of this late morning. The glass container says it is the scent of tobacco. I think of my father's occasional cigar. And across the street, where hammers had been striking pointy steel for hours, there is now nothing, only a cold quiet, like the kind that often comes on a night in winter.

The drive to the library is in the dark. Only 5:45 p.m. but the air and the shadows make it appear much later. The GPS on the phone maps a circuitous route, avoiding stretches on the busy tollway. The library is only 15 miles from my home, but in these hours of the day the traffic mocks time. My phone indicates it will be nearly an hour before I arrive, later than I had planned.

I am moderating—along with another local writer—a discussion about Hemingway's *A Moveable Feast*. It is part of a series the local Hemingway Foundation is presenting. Hemingway was born in Oak Park, just outside of Chicago, and the locals here take pride in that, no matter what kind of man they might think Hemingway was. The crowd is expected to be a good size, maybe four dozen or so. I take the main road from home to the state highway and head north. Headlights surround me. The night is cold but not as cold as it had been earlier in the week, so I wear only a light jacket. Too light for a long walk; just right for auto travel. I have prepared little for this talk, other than to reread Hemingway's book of his early years in Paris, a book I had read at least five times. I had forgotten how controversial and funny it is in places. Humor is not something many think about when they think of old Ernie. I hope to offer up those thoughts tonight, but also the deeper issues about migration and expats and how that fits in a modern world where immigrants and refugees are commonly scorned. There is also the question of age. Hemingway wrote this book in his final years when his health was waning, and his mental stability was in question. There's been so much documentation about the oncoming of his dementia in the late 1950s when he gathered his old notes from the days in the French capital with Pound and Fitzgerald and sat down to pen what he had remembered.

What did he *really* remember? What did his aging and battered brain allow him to recollect? How true is a memory, especially one from a vulnerable mind? And yet, what does it matter, really? In the preface to *A Moveable Feast*, Hemingway suggests: "If the reader prefers, this book may be regarded as fiction." He is implying that all on these pages may not be journalistically true. He completes his preface by writing that his recollections, however you might label them, nevertheless "may throw some light on what has been written as fact."

I turn off the expressway toward the library and my phone rings. I don't recognize the number and normally wouldn't answer, but it is past the time I told those at the library that I would arrive and so maybe someone is checking on my whereabouts.

"This is David."

"Hey, it's Keith. Just checking that you're on your way."

Keith is with the Hemingway Foundation.

"Yes. Just around the corner."

"You know it's at the Maze library, right?"

"Yep. All good. Just a few minutes."

I reminded myself of the location earlier today and noted it on my phone's calendar. There was a time when being a few minutes late would put me in a foul mood. I'm beyond that now. The start of the talk is still 25 minutes away. My fellow writer and I had previously spoken about what we believed might be good discussion topics. And I'm not interested in mingling more than I must. I'm not opposed to it, but long sessions turn into awkward moments and odd conversations.

The library from the outside looks like a 1940s elementary school, stone and brick and concrete with large arched windows. The double wooden door squeaks when I open it.

"I'm here for the Hemingway event," I say to the young woman at the checkout desk.

## 7

"Sure. Downstairs in the meeting room."

I walk around the large, battered oak desk, dodging piles of books on the floor. At the stairs, there are empty boxes and crates piled waist high. The hallway smells of mildew and dust. The walls are a dirty yellow. Despite the love it appears to need, this building, this library, is clearly one that is used, frequented, and maybe even beloved for what it has been and become. It has earned its age spots.

For nearly two hours we talk joyously about Paris, and seriously about migration, and refugees, and expatriates. We talk about artist communities and how Laurel Canyon in the early 1970s may have sprouted the same creative seeds as France in the 1920s. When my colleague and I find ourselves drifting down a parallel road toward George Orwell's *Down and Out in Paris and London*, we are sternly routed back to Hemingway by a slightly perturbed man in the back row, peering over his thick black glasses, reminding us why we are here—Hemingway, Fitzgerald, Pound, Picasso, Gertrude Stein. And through it all, reminding us of what we knew, that Hemingway wrote the book in his late years as he suffered from mental anguish. And with that, as I had considered earlier, we discuss the mystery of memory, and when we begin to lose the capacity to recollect how we tussle in the murky shadows between what was then and what is now. "The present is where we live while the past is where we dream," wrote John Banville in his memoir, *Time Pieces*. But when we awake, we don't always remember our dreams, recalling only fragments of them in the late hours of the day; some flicker as one as we fly over the sea or walk into an unfamiliar room lined with books. On my drive home, I could only wonder what dreams I have had that I have never remembered, dreams lost in the void created by the mundane tasks of living—washing pans, dusting shelves, sorting the mail—or in the deeper emptiness that slowly encases you after the loss of a loved one or the sneaky passing of youth, unnoticed until the ashes are scattered.

When I arrive home, I cannot sleep. I eat half a banana, drink water, and take the dog out in the backyard to do her business. Just behind and above me in the tall trees, resounding in the vague tangle of high branches, is the night call of a bird. It's a curious song. I've heard it before in dark hours like these, a tone that is peculiarly bright. Not an owl. Not a hawk, several of which nest in the ancient trees along the road. Why does it sing its song? Why now? Is it protection? Defense? Is it calling for a mate, a ballad of longing? I don't pretend to know, but smile in the direction of the odd twitter, certain, if nothing else, that it is much like Whitman's song, one of celebration. For this bird, like Hemingway to the end, has remembered how to live.

# 8

My friend calls from Kansas. He says he can see again.

There have been several operations, months of not being able to read, and certainly no driving. Walking with cautious, tentative steps, straining to look at the world and notice its tiny beauties but seeing only haze. Hospitals hundreds of miles away. Doctors and specialists. And now with unique lenses in a pair of new frames, my friend sees more than shadows and glints of light. He sees his wife's loving face, he sees his own in the mirror, he sees the delicate shades of purple in the lavender plants he cultivates on his farm, he sees the coming days.

It has been a long haul, yet still, there may be complications to come—more doctors and more specialists. There had been detached retinas that might happen again. But on this day, he can see, and he is blessed, he says. Blessed by some higher power. Some force others might call God. Blessed by fate or the fortunes of spirits unknown, and he has telephoned, he says, just to let me know.

I had taken my phone with me and sat on a soft chair in the solitude of my wife's office to listen to his words. Now, after saying goodbye, I sit motionless, the phone on my lap. My wife stirs something in a metal pot on the stove. The radio is tuned to the news. The dog wrestles with a squeaky chew toy. Yet, in my head it is quiet. Stillness has overtaken me, my muscles limp, sensing only the in and out of my breath. On the desk is a photograph of my stepdaughter and stepson. They are young, smiling, sitting together near a pier. It appears to be somewhere in Europe, maybe. I did not know them then, but I see that moment now and I am grateful. I enter the bedroom and on the west wall is an enlarged photograph of a tree-lined path in France. My son took this photo many years ago on a trip with his mother. The photographer's point of view is purposely askew, the vision not perfectly centered. I like to think he took this image believing that nothing in life is truly balanced—not a path, not a gardener's planted trees, not in the way we see what is before us.

It is difficult to understand how the eyes work, a mystery of lens and light and electrical impulses that are carried by the optic nerve to the brain. Complex refractions that somehow give us shapes and colors. But more than this, the eyes are our souls. And to see with them is to see oneself in the world. To look in the eyes of others can only be described as magical. Voltaire is believed to have said that the mirror is a worthless invention and that "the only way to see yourself is in the reflection of someone else's eyes." If there is no sight, the mind must search for another way to recognize the love of a wife, a friend, a son, a daughter, and to discover who they are, for Voltaire's worthless mirror is just that, worthless. Not seeing is not knowing. It is darkness far beyond the lack of light.

I return to the kitchen, and at the edge of the granite counter I stop for a moment and watch my wife, her back to me as she works at the sink. Her shoulders rise and fall. And in the window beyond her, an impressionistic image is captured in the glass along with the evening shadows of the trees beyond her reflection, creating a fleeting, muted portrait that I see only in a flash of time, an image of beauty and home, an image that quickly falls away as my wife moves out of the soft lamplight above her and night devours the final seconds of day.

# 9

The gray that seeps through the curtains is deep and yet murky like the light in a scene from an old movie. It must be quite early. I roll over and nestle against a pillow, not about to return to sleep — I like it here. I am alone and it is a good place to linger. After all, it must be at least an hour before sunrise, and it's my birthday.

Eventually, I become curious, and I reach for my phone. It is later than I had thought. Nearly 7 a.m. That seems impossible. There is also a text on the screen from my younger son. The words sent sometime overnight. *I love sharing my birthday with you*, he has written, *and wish there was a way I could share this with my future son or daughter. I love you like crazy dad. Happy birthday brother.* My son was born late at night on my thirty-sixth birthday. Gifts come in many ways.

My wife is already awake and dressed. She returns to the bedroom, leans into the sheets, and kisses me.

"It's your birthday," she says, her voice animated.

"That, it is," I mutter, not yet convinced of my morning footing.

In the bathroom mirror I see a man, one who is old with gray hair and tired eyes, yet this is a man who does not feel old. Yes, morning has yet to be shaken from these bones, but old is someone else. Not me. I angle closer to the glass and scratch my white beard, several days of growth. *I think I'll keep it for a while. I think I've earned it.* The reflection reminds me of a black-and-white photograph of a man I had recently seen in a story on the web about art in New Mexico. He is a painter who lives somewhere near the small town of Madrid. He carries unruly white hair and a scruffy snowy beard. His stare is intense. Sun-soaked skin. In a few months I hope to be in Los Cerrillos, the town just up the dusty road from Madrid. Maybe I can say hello.

I don't think much of my birthday anymore. Not that I don't like it, it is only that I am more indifferent than interested. It is not about aging, the slow and inevitable march, but instead it is the idea of time, that manmade concept. What does the counting of years really mean anyway? Still, my son's text and my wife's kiss are precious, and as I remain before the mirror, I am aware through my still weary eyes of the splendor of gratitude.

Before long, I'm in the shed. The space heater needs more time, so I'm bundled in fleece and a watchman's cap. A breeze is building. I hear a wind chime tingling and I write to the music. Through the window I see the last of the season's leaves on the grass, and in the distance, a neighbor has left a string of outdoor lights on through the night; the bulbs glow yellow in the bare trees. I am alone in the softness of it. Picasso said that without solitude, no serious work is possible. But solitude without time may instead be loneliness. Time can do that. In these early hours, although I write, the solitude before me is more meditation than work. It is a gift.

I return to the house. My wife has the radio on, the news on NPR. It's unsettling and hard to ignore the untruths and pandering of lawmakers and pundits. I tolerate it as I make coffee. This is *not* a gift, this news of the day. So, I shake from it and think of the casita in the Chihuahuan Desert along the Turquoise Trail south of Santa Fe, east of the Rio Grande, where prospectors once came to find gold, where the desert rose blooms, where the stars are impossible to count.

As my wife asks what I would like for my birthday dinner, my phone dings. *HAPPY BIRTHDAY!!!* The text is from my stepdaughter in Iowa. Another gift.

"I have those pork chops," my wife says.

"I could do that," I say.

"Or would you rather go out to eat? I know you like going out."

"Really, I'm good with what you decide."

"We could order pizza. Open some wine with it?"

Truth is, I don't want to decide. I don't want to make decisions. No decisions today. That would be a nice present.

"Surprise me," I say. "I'm sure your son will want something hearty."

My stepson is expected to join us.

By now, I have opened my computer on the kitchen counter to go through school emails before heading for the train. Facebook says there are 18 notifications. Last year, I was persuaded, I believe by my wife, to add my birthdate to my Facebook profile. I had been reluctant. "Don't you want people to wish you a good day?" she had asked. I have 18 good wishes on Facebook. Some from people I haven't spoken with in many years.

I catch the later train to the city and will arrive with just enough time to make a scheduled meeting in my department. But on the way, there's a schedule notification on my phone. The meeting is canceled. I am now traveling to nowhere and suddenly with nothing planned, an unexpected gift. When I arrive in the city, my mood changes, and on the short walk to the coffee shop I am mildly nauseated, slightly out of breath. When I had my heart attack several years ago, I had similar symptoms, but they included intense sweating and a heavy chest. I am experiencing neither this morning, and I keep my pace, but find myself wondering: *Who is it that gets to live a long life?* I was lucky with my attack. No damage to the heart. I could outlive my father by many years if I take care. Others, however, are not so lucky. Young people are shot dead in schools. Babies die of cancer. Yet, there are those who have abused their bodies for decades who keep on. Why would I expect this to make sense? Why would anyone say this is somehow God's will?

With only a block remaining on my walk to the café and still not feeling myself, my phone pings. I keep walking but glance at the screen. It's a long text from a former student. I order coffee and some brown toast, secure a seat, and read. Along with a happy birthday message is a detailed assessment of what he says I have meant to him, that I have not only been a teacher but a friend. I have inspired and steadied him. Supported and guided. *You made me cry*, I text back. *Mission accomplished*, he replies.

I'm thinking of the desert once again, and through a Google search find that Namib is the oldest desert in the world, some 80 million years. New Mexico's Chihuahuan is a baby. The age is unclear, different at each website, but it appears parts of the Chihuahuan are only a few million years old. It occurs to me that discovering the age of a desert must be such intricate work, taking years of study in ecology and geology. Later this spring when we are in Los Cerrillos, I hope to walk the scrappy ancient ground, step on long trails surrounded by agave and sage, and primeval rocks. It was a decade ago in Navajo Nation, in the high desert just outside the Grand Canyon, when I found myself moved by something beyond my comprehension. It was a cross-country journey with my sons, and we had spent the day walking the edge of the great gorge. Late in the day after traveling a few miles from the lodge at the North Rim, we arrived at a vista overlooking a vast open land of red and brown. In the warm breeze and under a mix of sun, silvery clouds, and a spitting drizzle, a double rainbow appeared at the expansive sky's highest point. The birds were silenced, the roaming cattle stilled. That moment was the envy of angels and I cried without fully understanding. Where I hope to find myself this spring is more than 500 miles east of where those angels had been, yet I will stand in the same ecosystem, the same prehistoric land as the Chihuahuan, and I will search beyond the Rio Grande to the distant mountains for the past and the future, and my heart will hunt the western sky for whatever it was that placed its tender hands on me ten years ago, opening me to the peace that only the ancients can bring.

After a few bites of toast and sitting quietly in the café, I feel better. The discomfort is gone. I am also at one of my favorite tables, near the south window in the corner, a spot that gives me joy, like resting in your favorite chair wrapped in a heavy quilt. And so, I write. And in the hours that pass I work to the clatter that surrounds me—honest voices and bits of laughter. There are clinking ceramic dishes and musical notes emanating from a speaker at the far end, notes nearly indiscernible in this familiar noise.

Midafternoon arrives and so has sunshine. I walk to the bookstore at the university building on State Street to search for a volume on New Mexico. The travel section is tucked behind the coffee bar. It takes me many minutes to discover the guides, and after endlessly searching the shelves, I find nothing on New Mexico. Not one book. There are guides for the entire American Southwest, Arizona, and Texas, but not specifically New Mexico. I search the travel-writing section. Nothing. It is as if New Mexico has been forgotten or dismissed. On the rack of folding maps there is Paris and New York and even a large map of Alaska, but again, nothing for Albuquerque, nothing for Santa Fe, nothing for New Mexico. Dismayed, I open my phone and order online a laminated map of what the poets call The Land of Enchantment. It will be delivered tomorrow, a gift to myself.

When I walk to the train later in the day for the ride home, the late November light is fading. I have spent most of this birthday alone. Not by myself, for that's impossible in the city, but still alone, alone in my thoughts and alone in my work. At the corner near Dearborn Street is a tiny old diner, or maybe it is made to look old to capture the imagination, I'm not certain. Still, at the window sits a man, maybe in his seventies, in a heavy coat and a brown fedora. He holds his coffee mug with both hands, his elbows on the counter before him. He is alone. A few blocks south of where I walk, on a wall at the Art Institute is what some have called the art world's most poignant image of American loneliness, Edward Hopper's *Nighthawks*. I can't help but think of that painting now, the man and woman at one end of the counter and another singular figure at the other, slumped over their coffees, the dark streets beyond them. Who is more alone, the couple or the man? And what about the one who sees this scene from across the street, the view of the painter? Isn't he, too, lonely? Undoubtedly, loneliness and aloneness are not the same. We assume that those in Hopper's image are isolated or forlorn. We would also believe, even if only for a moment, that the man I walked by in the diner on Dearborn is a lonely soul. Loneliness, in its truest sense, is all around us yet unremarkable and often undetectable, a product of the absence of connection or intimacy, hidden inside ourselves. Aloneness, the emotion that has carried my day, my birthday, is a different matter. With aloneness, I am in the presence of myself. When I was a kid, late into the night under the blankets of my bed, I listened to faraway signals on my transistor radio. I was the kid who read *Twenty Thousand Leagues Under the Sea* by flashlight and dreamed of immeasurable oceans. Alone. Not lonely. What an immense gift this is, this aloneness I carry now, walking late-autumn city streets in the creeping shadows of skyscrapers.

# 10

The horizon is red in the east. They say a sky like this means weather is on the way. Something is always on the way.

It is before dawn and my writing shed is chilly. I place the space heater near my bare legs under the table. It would have been better to pull on long pants. Shorts in the early morning of a late November day is my choice. No coffee, no food. Instead, I take the first few minutes of the day to snap a photo of the red sky, to pet the dog, and read a few emails. I see that my friend in Pittsburgh is ready to debut his documentary about Bruno Sammartino, the legendary wrestler. It is quite a story. I send congratulations. I see, too, that one of my students needs help posting her work to the school's portal. And there's an email from the nice woman who is coordinating my writing workshop next month for a group in Chicago's north suburbs. Writers have sent their work for review. I thank her.

For a moment, I am angry with myself. I did not erect this shed for these kinds of tasks. It is to be a sanctuary, not an office.

I light a candle and open my journal. There is a blank page and I have nothing yet to say. On my desk among the scattered books, below Karl Ove Knausgaard and Henry Miller is a volume of poems by Jim Harrison. It had been many years since I last read from this collection of verses. Last night, flipping through television channels, I found myself watching an old Anthony Bourdain episode, one of the *Parts Unknown* series. He was in Montana with Harrison, who lived in Big Sky country part of this life. In his creaky, halting, and breathy delivery, one born out of a long life of rich food, good wine, and cigarettes, Harrison offered his poetry and prose. *Time is a mystery that can flip us upside down*, he said. Not long after that episode, Harrison was dead. Bourdain is now dead, too.

I had plans to write this morning. Instead, I'm reading from Harrison's *Songs of Unreason* and thinking about heaven.

# 11

One of Andy Warhol's last works, *Camouflage*, was created a year before his death. The scale is massive, 9 feet tall and 35 feet wide, displaying a pattern that is both unnerving and all-encompassing. Brown and green blotches, the camouflage pattern of war used to disguise, vaguely obscure the image of Da Vinci's *Last Supper*.

My son is in town from Seattle. Thanksgiving is tomorrow and we are spending the afternoon at the Art Institute. The main exhibit is an immense Warhol collection. My son doesn't remember ever being at the museum when he lived here, something I find hard to imagine, so, we first hit the museum's highlights—Picasso's *Old Guitarist* and Seurat's *A Sunday Afternoon on the Island of La Grande Jatte*. We then spend two hours in the rooms that hold Warhol's images of soup cans and Coca-Cola, celebrity and tragedy, and camp. In the final room, the exhibit reveals—just as was done at the end of the artist's days—that Warhol had lived a life of secret piety.

Moving as close to the work as the guard will allow, I find the face of Jesus. It is there behind artistic concealment, Warhol's faith hidden yet apparent. It is said that nearly every day for many years, early in the morning, Warhol slipped into a back pew at St. Vincent Ferrer in New York. He spent Thanksgiving and Christmas at a soup kitchen. He helped put his nephew through seminary school. He carried a rosary in his pocket. Warhol was brought up Byzantine Catholic in his hometown of Pittsburgh and maintained his faith despite his image, despite the life at his studio—The Factory—where the hallmarks of the 1960s were evident—drugs, sex, and radical politics. Warhol never spiritually swayed from his Catholicism and its traditional tenets. Even as an openly gay man, he did not publicly support the gay movement. Many say it was because of his strict faith, and some say he made those daily visits to St. Vincent Ferrer to pray for forgiveness.

"He was a complicated man," I say to my son who stands beside me now before Warhol's work.

"A provocateur," my son adds.

In one's art, the layers are exposed, yet never truly explained. Warhol played up and on the American obsessions with money and fame. But was that a statement about him or about us? Who was Andy Warhol, really? Who are we, really?

Leaving the exhibit, my son wonders aloud about the idea of art. He wonders if blown-up silkscreen images, one of Warhol's trademark processes, are truly art or just a cheap vehicle. He's using someone else's image, my son says. That he did. But Warhol also used his own Polaroid pictures, I add. Is that art? I don't have the answer, but I argue that what we see as art is in how the images are used, how they are presented to the world. The art is in what we see and maybe in what we don't see. It is found in the mystery of things, deeper than face value, like Warhol himself.

Warhol's memorial service was held at New York's St. Patrick's Cathedral. It was a celebrity event that included Liza Minnelli, Calvin Klein, and Yoko Ono. The famous filled the church. But in the eulogy, his friend John Richardson reminded those who gathered that Warhol had fooled the world into believing he was consumed with fame, and what he was really doing was exposing society's appetites and revealing how we camouflage what's most important—our humanity. The real Andy Warhol and his art didn't truly come into focus until he was no longer there.

Standing inside the exit door, I detect a freshening wind outside and stop to pull my coat's collar to my chin to prepare for it.

"He was only 58 when he died," I say.

"And how did he die?"

"Heart issues, I believe."

When we leave this world, we will not know what will be left behind, what secrets will be unwrapped, what truths about ourselves unveiled. We can only hope to be who we are today, in the here and now, as honestly as we can.

To the left is the Art Institute's gift shop. My son nods toward it.

"You sure you don't want an Andy Warhol grilling apron or something?"

I shake my head and smile.

"But I kind of think maybe old Andy would have liked the idea of an apron with a superimposed image of his Marilyn Monroe."

We walk outside to the Institute's concrete steps. I am satisfied, believing I have untangled something, a kind of clandestine truth. From somewhere once hidden, I have an instant memory of my father drawing images of people on a napkin after a Sunday dinner, lingering at the dining-room table with a cup of coffee at his side, entertaining his boy with his pen. Draw me something cool, Dad, I would say. My father's artistry was a passion never fully realized. The faces he would create on the napkins were of men with sharp jaws and full heads of hair. Sometimes he would draw them smoking. My father loved to sketch in delicate lines, the smoke lifting from the tip of a cigarette. When Dad died, I found dozens of his drawings in a large envelope tucked away in a drawer, one of them a charcoal sketch of famous boxing champ Billy Cohn. My father loved boxing as a kid and revered the man they called The Pittsburgh Kid. Before me in this single image, on decades-old discolored and tattered drawing paper, was the evidence of two of my father's passions—art and sport. Dad did not hide either of these passions during his life, as Warhol did with the depth of his faith, but like all artists, secrets or not, my father had found what artists always seek—devotion.

My son and I begin our walk to the parking garage, trying to shield our faces from the wind between the skyscrapers. At the crosswalk at Jackson and Michigan, we wait in the biting chill for cars to pass, while the noisy city captures our senses like prisoners and refuses either of us the opportunity for independence. Yet, for a single moment my eyes are free, and I think I see my father waving from the other side of the avenue.

# 12

From the booth I see a dog—a Brittany Spaniel, it appears—
colors of caramel and eggshell, slipping its head out from the
slightly rolled-down back window of a dark-blue truck, the
dog's nose to the early morning sky. There is something sweet
in the air.

This small diner is a few blocks from home. It's been here
for decades. It has recently been remodeled—new booths and
chairs, new tiles on the walls—but it remains stuck in another
time. I order biscuits and gravy, scrambled eggs, and black
coffee in a ceramic mug, and the waitress, a woman of Polish
descent, smiles and asks the usual questions: Cream and sugar?
Fruit or toast? The truck with the dog inside is parked on the
street in front, and the dog's owners, a silver-haired woman and
a man in a green hunting jacket and a black cap sit on the other
side of the big window. They wave to the dog. They're watching
as it watches. Soon, the dog disappears deeper inside the truck.
It must know this routine.

There is no one in the diner under the age of 60, at least not
the patrons. The waitress might be in her forties. Christmas
music plays. A television hangs from the wall high above the
counter in the back where two men in flannel shirts sit silently
together. The TV is tuned to a morning news show, the sound
turned down. In the next booth, a man complains about his
adult daughter. His accent is that of a Chicagoan, stereotypical
in its flatness. "She's not grown up enough for a kid," he growls.
"She's not thinking straight," he says. The woman with him,
presumably his wife, nods.

I don't regularly order biscuits and gravy, but when it's
delivered, I am pleased. It's comforting, like this diner—familiar,
but not quite. The taste of the heavy food is rich and buttery, not

my usual breakfast flavors, just as the diner is not my usual spot. It is my first time here, although I've walked by countless times. As the waitress tops off my coffee without asking—a kind of compulsory gift—this, too, feels right and recognizable. And as others enter through the front door, old men, and women, those inside offer their good mornings by first name. Gary, Fred, and Margaret will also have their coffees topped off, familiar and expected. Unlike the others, no one knows my name here. Not today. Nonetheless, we share coffee from the same pot.

The poet Jim Harrison wrote about mornings like this. He comes to mind after the other night of reading. *Of late I see waking as another chance at spring.* Everyone inside these walls has awakened to find themselves in the company of memory, fueled by the breath of another day. In this morning, I am one of them. Despite the metal walker and the wooden cane left at the entrance, and the fake red carnations lightly covered in dust in the old ivory vase at the checkout counter, I am young among the old, an old they do not know, an old they might reject or cannot diagnose. Just as the others are, I, too, am reaching toward spring.

As I stand to pay my bill and exit, the dog is again visible through the glass, its nose peeking from the truck's window, searching for that sweet smell again, the familiar one it sought earlier, the one it may not have found just yet, or maybe the one it yearns to rediscover from somewhere long ago.

# 13

It is early on a December day, before light, and my phone dings. There is a text from a family member, a photo of a pregnant young woman, a screenshot from a Facebook post. She is standing next to her smiling partner, her hand on her belly. It is the daughter of an old friend, a friend I have not talked to in a very long time. He has been distant for years. I was the best man at his second wedding, and he was invited to mine, but never came. I had heard of this news, this pregnancy, but despite my old friend and the two of us watching our children grow up together, despite the family pool parties, despite all our travels—a long cross-country trip along Kerouac's roads— despite our prolonged conversations over bottles of red wine when lives were seemingly falling apart, despite late-night calls of desperation and afternoon laughter about life's unexpected turns, despite being much younger together, despite all the years, he disappeared.

The words accompanying the photo text suggest a baby shower was held and that her father, my old friend, did not attend. Curious and complicated, I wonder. For a moment, I accept the ache of missing him, and lean against the kitchen counter in the emerging light of the morning to consider what winter will bring, this season of inky darkness that often comes with remarkably clear nights, where answers wait while the world sleeps off the hangovers of autumn and summer. The coldest time of year is nearing, but it will eventually restore us and bring warmer days, and like the seasons with my old friend, it, too, will come to an end.

# 14

The old bookshop in Edinburgh is no longer for sale and my dream is a not a dream anymore. It is someone else's.

I sit at the small dining table, tending to student grades, and for whatever reason I am reminded of that tiny corner bookstore near the university that had been for sale earlier this year. It stood out on Hope Park Crescent with its green-painted stone front among the gray of the surrounding buildings along the old road.

*What ever happened to Tills?*

A search of the web proves it has been purchased by Kate and Joshua McNamara for somewhere around $176,000. Fully stocked with all the books. The original owners who ran it for decades—Rick and Ann—seemed such lovely people. The email I sent months ago inquiring about the place was greeted with warmth. They wanted to be sure the next owners would nurture what had been their life's passion. *We've had a lot of interest,* Ann wrote to me. *Many find the dream of running an old bookshop in Edinburgh very appealing,* she added.

Images of the shop on the web show stacks of books, tall shelves, and a fireplace, reminding me of what I have allowed to pass by. There is such glorious romanticism in the idea. But despite this, Ann also wrote in her reply email: *However, practicalities must prevail.* She also included a document detailing all the financial particulars. I read it five times the day the note came, and then asked my wife what she thought.

"Depending on what happens in the election, I'd go in a heartbeat," she said.

"Tills would be gone by then," I said. "Someone is going to jump on this."

And someone has. I blinked. Missed it. Lost it. I find more images on the internet and stare. *Would I have really done this? Could I? Scotland. Edinburgh. Books in the UNESCO City of Literature.* I would embrace the community, wear a tweed jacket, and take my lunches at the pub down the road. There would be morning tea made with hot water taken from a kettle left on the bookstore stove. I'd smile at the customers and help them find Burns, Robert Louis Stevenson, Doyle, and Muriel Gray. There would be a bookstore dog. Customers would know the name.

My dog puts her head on my lap, and I pat her nose. We couldn't have brought her with us; I would have been concerned about the long plane flight. Not sure traveling over the Atlantic by air with a dog is permitted, doable, or safe.

My wife is awake now. I hear her steps from the bedroom, and put water on the stove for her coffee.

"Tills is gone," I say.

"What was that?"

"The bookstore in Scotland, it sold."

She stops in the hallway to pet the dog.

"Oh. Well, not surprising."

"Locals, I think."

"Are you sad?"

"I am. I really think I am."

The kettle whistles and I turn off the burner. *What is it that has me sad? A simple missed opportunity? Or is it something else?* Through the kitchen window I see the breeze move the low branches of the magnolia tree. *Melancholy is a longing based in silly romanticism.* I wonder if some dreams are to remain just that—dreams. But here I am, the years counting on, with this once magical possibility before me, and instead of moving on it, I settle. *Is that what this is?* When we are young, we imagine these opportunities and many of us take action. When we are old, we default to the safe and secure, giving in to the mundane or familiar when time is diminishing. This morning, that equation does not calculate.

I pour coffee beans into the grinder and turn it on, pour hot water in the press, and set a mug near it in front of my wife, who has now taken a seat at the counter.

"Do you remember that story, some article somewhere, about the *other* bookstore—not Tills—where you could stay and run the place for a time? You rent it and stay in the rooms above. Remember that?"

"Wasn't that Scotland, too?"

Another internet search turns up a small bookstore in Wigtown in the Galloway region. I show images to my wife of whitewashed buildings and seaside cottages in a town with a population of only 1000 but 15 bookstores. One of them is The Open Book.

"You remember this?" I ask.

There is urgency to my question, but my wife's questions are practical. She does remember this place.

"So, when? Do we fly to Glasgow? How much does it cost to stay there? And remind me, do you actually run the place?"

"Yes. You have some help. But yes, you are the bookseller for however long you decide."

"And how long would you decide?"

Two weeks seems right to me, maybe more. One week is not enough to truly settle in. I turn again to the internet and read more about the process, renting, and running the place. Delight wells up. I am as buoyed as I was when I first considered Tills.

"We have New Mexico in a few months," my wife reminds me.

The spiritual land. The remoteness. The ache of nature. My mind, for a moment, shifts to the desert.

"We could do both," I say. "The bookstore is filled up for several years straight. There would be time. Many months between now and then. I could save up for expenses. And in the meantime, place our names on a waiting list."

I send an email to the Association of Wigtown Booksellers and, for the hell of it, search the web for other bookstores for sale in Scotland.

# 15

The discussion turns to heritage.

"Wait, I'm Welsh?" The question comes from my wife.

It is a late-morning birthday breakfast for my father-in-law at a local diner. There is coffee and pancakes and eggs. My mother-in-law has a sandwich, as it's after 11 a.m. The talk turns to family and lineage, and when I say I might want to try one of the popular DNA kits to confirm my Irishness and Englishness and Germanness, my mother-in-law reminds her husband that there is a bit of Wales in his background. My wife is confused.

"I thought we were English," she says.

Her mother clarifies that, yes, there is English. But on the other side, my father-in-law's side, there is also Welsh.

"I had no idea," my wife says.

But the DNA kit does not interest my wife in the same way that it does me. I want to know more about my mother's family who worked the stables at Osbourne House on the Isle of Wight. I want to know more about my Irish Catholic great-grandmother who lived in a Protestant Ireland. And there are many unknowns to the German side. Genetic pasts are our DNA ambigrams, pieces of our DNA viewed in different ways, interpreted by how the viewer sees them. I want to see those pieces through my own eyes.

"I think there's some Eastern European in there somewhere, too, but no one talked about that, for whatever reason," I say.

My mother told me stories of her family emigrating from England, her father coming to America to work as an ice boy, carrying blocks of ice up steep Pittsburgh stairs at the age of 13. But they were just tales of people I never knew. Now, I'm longing for some mysterious connection, some rooted familial context to a life. I am likely to be surprised, and maybe results of a DNA test will derail long-held truths. I'm sure there are secrets in those genes. My maternal grandmother disappeared for several years when she was a young woman, a fact that wasn't revealed until after her death when the funeral home discovered her birth certificate did not square with the age she had claimed. Did she have a baby out of wedlock? Young women disappeared regularly for this reason all those years ago. I know a DNA kit cannot answer this question, but the same curiosities that feed that query feed so many others.

We ask for coffee refills and wonder aloud about the mongrels that most of us are, clinging to purebreds, surnames linked to ancient lands on the other side of the world, places we have never been. Around us in the diner are others in groups of family and friends who, in varying degrees, are also connected by blood to those whom they have never seen. Yet, for most, there is some level of pride and comfort in the knowledge that we belong.

On the ride home, my father-in-law, sitting in the front seat with my wife at the wheel, opens his birthday present—a calendar of classic military planes—then his card.

"What's this?" He points to the number written inside the card and looks at his daughter.

"Your age," she says.

He appears puzzled.

"Eighty-nine," my wife adds. "You're 89."

He shakes his head.

"I'm 88."

My wife is surprised and maybe a little embarrassed.

"I thought you were 89. I'm so sorry. Why did I think you were 89?"

That night as I lie in bed and my wife sleeps at my side, I smile thinking how she had forgotten the age of her father. Not because it was odd or awkward, but because it wasn't.

There are many days I must count the years to recall the ages of my sons, my wife, my dog, even to calculate my own age on occasion. Strange, maybe, but no stranger than believing I am genetically tied to a small village in Ireland or Germany, or a cemetery on the Isle of Wight where the names of ancestors are carved on gravestones. I am, and all of us are, the places where our ancestors have lived and died, and we are every age we have ever been. We carry it all. There is an undeniable part of us that lives outside of time, reminded of age only in unexpected remarkable moments.

# 16

The book is delivered in a plain brown wrapper, a used edition purchased online from a small secondhand store somewhere in the American West for a few pennies and a couple of dollars to cover the cost of shipping. The book is one I have been anticipating. In the shed, I sit in the leather chair and look around me. Books on two small shelves, books stacked 15 high on my desk, books on the floor. If I died today, all of this would be my epitaph; it would say much about me, more than any formal eulogy might. And this one, the book delivered this morning, would certainly expose my current state of mind.

Shaun Bythell, rather unexpectedly, bought a used bookstore in Wigtown more than a decade ago. He wrote about his daily life there as a book merchant. *The Diary of a Bookseller* caught my eye when researching Wigtown. The book received good reviews when it was released, and it seems exactly the read for right now.

The leather chair is cold. The heater struggles to do its job to keep the shed reasonably warm in the few remaining cold days of autumn. So, I wear my wool watch cap. It's been frigid lately and it is again today. *I wonder what rural southwest Scotland is like in the winter. That old stone bookstore must have a fireplace, no?* The book is written in diary form marked by the days—how many customers per day, how many books sold. A few pages in, Bythell writes of his unanticipated connection to The Open Book, the one where my name is now on the waiting list. I feel a connection with him, as odd as that may sound.

Yesterday I received word of two friends of mine who have had their lives turned upside down by upheaval in their jobs. One is now out of work, another's pay drastically cut. What will they do? Ride it out? Work as baristas? I wonder if this had happened to me at this moment in my life if I would work harder at finding a way to get myself to Wigtown or, maybe, to New Mexico. That, too, is on my mind. Retirement? No. That word, that concept, seems out of step. It rings of old-fashioned values and misplaced dreams.

I read on.

It is clear Bythell is happy, whatever that means. It comes across on the pages. But could this be literary license? His words are clear. Bookselling, he writes, is not what the romantics say it might be. And he often quotes George Orwell, who worked in a bookshop for a time, and who seemed cranky about it—the surly customers, their lack of knowledge of real literature, the utter un-bookishness of those who would peruse for hours and buy nothing. Still, despite some minor evidence of Bythell being a bit of a curmudgeon, there is joy between the lines on these pages. Or am I only hoping it is there?

It was February in the year Bythell began the diary, and I read now what he writes about Wigtown in the winter—brutal. Sideways rain. *I'm sure it doesn't get as cold as it is here today in Chicago.* I pull my watch cap over my ears and check the space heater.

It is now March in the book's storyline. I break and look again at the shelves that surround me. My boyhood bedroom was like this, books all around. Volumes of *World Book Encyclopedia,* a gift from my parents in my early years, were lined in alphabetical order on a shelf above my bed. I remember sitting on the floor, reading about dinosaurs and deep ocean creatures, about George Washington and Thomas Jefferson. On another shelf were The Hardy Boys and Dr. Seuss. Books about birds and reptiles and dogs sat on a lower shelf. There was also my mother's bookshelf in her bedroom. Books on British history, kings, and queens. *David Copperfield, Peyton Place,* and several volumes on the Kennedys. Reading was of a different sort for my father. He read golf magazines almost exclusively, and in the home's basement he kept a two-shelf cabinet where hundreds of his personal copies of *Golf Digest* were neatly stacked and meticulously categorized by date.

Maybe there is something to all of this, attempting to answer the question of why I long for Wigtown. There's no Scottish in my blood, not that I know of, but the United Kingdom is in the genes, certainly. Books are and always have been part of daily life — those books of my boyhood and all the books in my current home and here in the shed. Golf's origins are in the United Kingdom, too. I love the game. My father loved the game.

I fold over the page to mark where I will resume my reading at a later time, and before I step out of the shed, I notice a ragged hardback book on the shelf by the door, a biography of Dickens. It was my mother's, a gift from me many years ago. It is mine now.

Mom would have loved to walk the streets and browse the bookshops of Wigtown.

# 17

It is an hour before dawn on the day of the winter solstice. Longest night of the season is nearing its end as the waning crescent moon hangs in the southeastern sky. I stand in the backyard in my olive barn coat and cap, the dog beside me, and look up through the exposed black trees to see it shine. It is remarkably clear this early morning, so much so that I detect the earth's shadowy rim. Quiet, too, only a far-off train chugging westward to a new destination. The last few days have been this way, moving toward something new. For weeks daylight has been diminishing, folding into longer nights, and now this morning, when the sun rises in the light of the first full day of winter, everything will begin to change.

Farther to the rear of the yard is where in autumn I planted tulip bulbs. The ground is now hard. But underneath the crusty dirt, even in these dark first hours of a new season, those bulbs are turning over, readying for what is to come. Many of us complain how winter lasts forever, but that is only a matter of obsession with the thermometer. Cold and darkness do not stop the endless patterns of life.

"Do you see the moon?" I ask my dog in a whisper.

The dog appears to have her eyes toward the sky.

I take out my phone for a photo, but the moon is impossible to capture. Besides, what is before me will not last and I cannot save it. For three days, the moon will slowly disappear, and at the same time the sun will rise and set at virtually the same place on the horizon. In Latin, solstice means "the standing still of the sun." This alignment in the sky, while the earth continues to adjust to a new moon, is the symbol of the start of a fresh beginning. The new moon is sometimes called an "old man." But it is not there yet. This morning the moon is at the end of its waning phase, and that, for now, is an invitation to surrender, to detach, to think things over.

Slowly walking south and then east, I am again struck by the silence. My sense of sight is the most dominant. Christmas bulbs from nearby homes light the way before me, as there are no streetlamps here. A string of lights tied around a large tree softly blink, and there are reflections of decorated holiday trees through wide living-room windows. All of this shifting my focus, for a few moments, from that extraordinary moon. But then there it is once more, above tall branches, with just enough shine to delicately illuminate a stream of clouds to the north. Simultaneously, this hour before dawn is both a symbol of time running out and of time still to come, of what is behind and what is forward. The crescent moon—more than 230,000 miles away from the earth—is a morning moon, in the sky since 3:00 a.m., and one that will remain there until it sets in mid-afternoon. It, too, is a disappearing moon, offering all of itself in the time it has left in the light of day.

I am uncertain where the phrase "thin places" originated, this description of the special destinations of spiritual degree. This moment is such a place, a "thin place," where one is hypnotized by a sense of grace—a space, it has been said, that lies in the fractures between heaven and earth. And in this place, I can continue unabated, but only along this path illuminated under this moon. If I turn north, the moon will be at my back and out of sight. So, I continue to move south and then east and then south again for nearly an hour with the moon visible always. The walk comes at the time of the season when one of the earth's poles is angled at its maximum distance from the sun, and there is total darkness in the north. There is only one way to travel—toward the illuminated sphere, south and east, the truest passage to take at this hour on this day in this astonishing light.

# 18

I wish I had known John Damp and been there to witness the way he and his wife Alice managed all those children—23 of them, all single births, all born and raised on the Isle of Wight. How in heaven did they wrangle them all?

John was a coachman and worked, I've been told, at least part of his days for the Royal Family at their residence on the Isle. Alice worked in the kitchen of the royal residence. How did they find the money, the time, the energy to feed all those children? Somehow they did, because there they are in the center of this remarkable photograph, smiling and waving to the camera while their children and their children's children wave, too.

"This is the photo my mother told me about," I say to my son, the two of us sitting at the kitchen counter.

"And there it is," he says.

"And right there is Nanny," I say, pointing to the dark-haired little girl in the center of the photo.

A young girl in the middle of the first row holds my 1-year-old mother in her arms.

The photo, it has been said, was taken for *Life* magazine in 1935, but probably not, since the magazine's first edition wasn't published until late 1936. Maybe another magazine? Regardless, the photograph is remarkable—a family reunion, a newsworthy one at that. Not all the family is there, but most are. If they had been, the camera might not have been able to frame them all. The grainy black-and-white photo doesn't permit me to clearly see the eyes of those looking at the lens, but I can see smiles, and I can see joy.

DNA-testing analysis came as a holiday gift, just as I had hoped. Although I have not yet sent in a sample, the kit is allowing me to log on to a website that would assist in tracking my family. I begin with my mother's side—the Warrens. My grandfather was born on the Isle of Wight to George and Ada Damp. Census documents and research by other family members tell of my grandfather's days as a truck driver, his meager yearly salary of just over $1000 in 1940, about $18,000 in today's money. I discover his death certificate. He was 51 years old. He died of a hemorrhage caused by heavy drinking.

"These are the same words on my sister's death certificate," I say.

"Exact same?" my son asks.

"Exact."

There is another photo of the Warren brothers and their wives—all so young. The men are dressed in jackets and ties, the women in dresses, some smoking, all smiling. The research someone has entered on the site reads, "The Warren men were all very handsome and all hard drinkers."

"It appears no one left the Isle of Wight to come to America for a long time," my son says.

The document list of the Damps is long, all of them born and bred on the Isle.

"My grandfather was quite young when he came to America," I say.

One document shows he arrived at Ellis Island with his mother when he was only a few years old, and notes in the research suggest he started work in the US at the age of 10, carrying blocks of ice. I had heard he was around 13 when he started working, but it appears he was younger.

My family tree has roots in England, and I see this before me, but there is also lineage from Ireland and Germany. In time, I will search those out and discover where the links lead. In the meantime, I'll send a sample of my saliva and wait for the DNA results.

"I don't suspect there will be any big surprises," I say.

"You never know," my son says.

Maybe it is age that breeds curiosity on these matters.

"Maybe I'm Navajo," I joke.

My son rolls his eyes. I think again about the coming trip to New Mexico and the visit to the Navajo Nation years before.

A few days ago, on Christmas night around the dinner table with my son, his mother, my wife, and the last of the holiday wine, the conversation had turned to the topic of death. The subject had morphed in that direction from talk of past Christmases and family members who were no longer with us. We shared wishes of how we want to be remembered, memorial services or not, and songs to be played or not. There was nothing morbid or sad about any of this. We wondered aloud about death itself, about where the soul goes—if there is one—and if memorials matter when the one whose life you are remembering is not there to appreciate it. Memorials are for the living, we all agreed. Now, days later with part of my family's history in front of me, with generational eyes looking back at me from this website that has documented my ancestry, I see my son studying the photos just as I am, wondering like me, how he might fit in, where his own spirit lies, what ancient ties are tangled in his blood. And as night darkens the room and the only light that remains comes from the edges of the single kitchen lamp just above our heads, I can hear my mother's voice reminding me that nothing lasts forever.

# 19

It is New Year's Eve morning, and it has snowed. Through the kitchen window, I see untouched white groundcover glistening in the lights above the garage door. The inside house lights remain off even though it is too early for the sun. I turn on my book light and sit in the leather chair with two volumes, one to finish and one to begin. The outside cold is seeping through the wall at the bay window and my bare feet are chilled. The kind of quiet that only snowfall allows is broken momentarily by a plow grinding its blade along the street, but even this does not disturb. The dog sleeps in a parallel chair, unmoved by the sound of the plow, and my eyes and my attention remain steady on the page before me.

I want to finish *The Diary of a Bookseller* this morning and return to a collection of George Orwell's essays, a volume I began two days ago. *How will the diary end*, I wonder? The author remains the shop's proprietor to this day, so his bookseller story continues. In pages near the end, he mentions for the second or third time the nearby bookstore—The Open Book, the Airbnb where one can stay and run the bookstore. *The Diary of a Bookseller* was published three years ago and even then, the author had written about the success of The Open Book. Its popularity is only broader now and the Wigtown Book Festival has grown along with it. I wonder if the booking page has new available dates. The New Year certainly must mean there are available times.

The usual New Year's celebration is planned for tonight, a quiet dinner at home—good wine, filets, lobster tail, and Brussels sprouts. My wife has already put out the good dishes, and I'll soon prepare the spices and the pots and pans, so when it's time to cook, which I'll be doing, it will be an easier go of it. We will talk at dinner about the past year and what's to come—our travels, and what we hope for in the months ahead. "Death Night" will also come up in the conversation. We need to document our wishes. We don't want it to be someone else's burden. So much has been said between the two of us on this subject, but nothing has been formalized. More importantly, it is time to tend to our wills. We've put this off far too long. Maybe we can secure some dates and check this off the list soon. All this is in my head now after reading the final diary entries in the bookseller's book, each one about bookstore customers who have passed away.

Looking through the blinds at the window, I'm surprised at how dark it still is. *Aren't the days getting longer now?* A streetlight shimmers across the branches of a snow-covered tree. What a lovely sight despite the darkness all around. It's wonderful to sit here in the early hours, two books before me, the dog, the house so silent with a new decade in front of us, a time of renewal and rebalance. I hate resolutions, but reflection is another matter.

Returning to the book's last pages, I wonder, as I have many times through the course of these recent days: *Could I truly run off and run a used bookstore?* When Orwell did it part-time, he found so much that was less than ideal. The diary's author has continually written of similar revelations. But, like Orwell, he cannot dismiss his duties or abandon them. On the final page, the author reflects on how he will continue to do "whatever is required to keep the ship afloat," and resolves to continue. Closing the book, I open my computer to check for any available new dates for The Open Book. There is nothing until 2023. The proprietor also asks those booking to pay upfront, no matter how many years in advance. Something I am not prepared to do. Instead, I again add my name to the waitlist using a different email, hoping that might offer some advantage, and switch to the Orwell book and his first essay about his days as a young man at a snobbish academy and his insatiable love of reading.

# 20

Sitting still at the dining table is a pleasure on this first day of the New Year. It is early evening now, and through the south window I see the street corner illuminated by a single streetlamp. I'm searching the web for an old poem. In the New Year, I have pledged to learn to recite three verses by memory. Frost's "Dust of Snow" and Yeats' "When You Are Old" are easy to find, but the third takes a few more clicks and pursuits, as only two of the poem's stanzas are popping up, not the entire work.

Auden's "As I Walked Out One Evening" came to me when finishing the Wigtown bookstore diary. The author had tried to learn it by heart. It is a remarkable poem, tangling love and the confines of time together in a way that reminds one of how precious the days are on earth. *Why not learn the poem?* The first stanzas brought me to tears and I wanted more. In time, I find the entire poem, copy and paste it into a document, title it Poems to Memorize, and save it to my desktop.

A friend of a friend can recite long sections of Dylan Thomas' "A Child's Christmas in Wales," delivering it with such passion that Thomas himself might be awestruck. I think of him now, that friend of a friend. *How did he make that commitment? And why, other than the story's sheer beauty?* On almost every New Year's Day, you find yourself considering the things that you have secretly, sometimes for a very long time, always wanted to do. *Is it finally time to do it? Still, when you initially act upon what it is you hope to accomplish, do you not also know that it, too, will soon fade like so many other wants and desires you have resolved to take on?* This I wonder as I read Auden's poem. "The clocks had ceased their chiming," are his words, "And the deep river ran on."

What have I been, in all these years? What am I now as the river runs on? These are questions for others to answer, not for me. Yet, sitting here in the quiet, reading the poems, I consider what I want to be in the time that is left. I'm not an old man in modern terms. The sixties might be the new forties, some say. Yes, it is true that time is running out. But it always has been. Time and its passage have been a constant undertow, pulling us out to sea, and we have been swimming against the tide since the day of our birth. None of this is extraordinary thinking, but this is what is before me tonight, and in the moment, it holds something deep.

Out of curiosity, I search websites for statistics on daylight. Since the solstice last month, the world has gained just under four minutes of sunlight. *More light is good for us, right?* It is healthy. It soothes us. There are studies that say that the view through a hospital window and the exposure to the natural light that pours in helps us heal. But without night, there is no day. So, yes, the growing days shine more light on us, but the nights cannot be forgotten or dismissed. Out the window, and across the lighted corner, is a home bright in holiday glow — red and green lights. Without the night, that view, that experience, is lost. Experience, in dark or light, is still just that, experience. And, without falling into some tired old mantra, it occurs to me that what I do, what we all do with the experience of night and day — dark and light — is what ultimately matters. In the time that is left, in the waning light that comes with winter and pushes toward the springs of the years remaining, it is clearer now what it is I want to do. I wish to release myself from the clichés of a modern life, and discover newness, away from the expected and anticipated, and toward grounded joy that allows an evolution from what I used to be while fundamentally being who I am. This is a choice. Like choosing those three poems to memorize; like knowing by heart what is important.

This summer I will travel to Seattle to see my older son. We will take a cooking class together and walk his dog in the fir-filled mountains of the Pacific Northwest. I will book those dates tomorrow along with a trip to Arizona with my stepson to play golf. I will phone my younger son to see how his New Year's house party got along, and the two of us will laugh about how silly the celebrations can be. And I will finalize whatever remains to be done for that trip under the wide sky of the New Mexico desert.

# 21

At the kitchen counter, I read the news and a few Twitter posts. A friend has tweeted that World War III is upon us and makes a joke that it might be best just to take a nap. A US airstrike has killed an Iranian commander at Baghdad's airport, and now the headlines tell me thousands more US troops are being deployed to the Middle East. That proposed nap might produce a nightmare.

Despite the news, I move forward, send emails to colleagues at the college, and reach out to writers and reviewers who have offered to blurb a novel of mine due out in the spring. Breakfast comes under new parameters to cleanse my body, and I read a post about a 21-day food challenge program. There's a story about Alex Trebek's final *Jeopardy* show, and his battle with terminal cancer. In a West Sumatra forest, scientists have discovered the world's largest flower — 4 feet in diameter. And on the front page of the *New York Times* there is more about the coming elections, an election with the oldest presidential candidates in the history of the nation.

My wife is clearing out the refrigerator, stacking old jars on the counter.

"Should we keep this?" she asks.

She has opened a container holding roasted Italian peppers.

"Hmm. That doesn't look so good," I say.

She places it on the far end of the counter near the sink.

"What about this?" she asks.

It's another jar of something, its identity uncertain.

"That should go," I say.

Old stuff, all of it outlasting better times.

As my wife continues to purge, I return to the news and social media. A friend who was dismissed from her journalist's job has found another; one better suited, it seems, at this stage of her life and career. She has posted to Twitter what she believes is a T. S. Eliot quote: "What we call the beginning is often the end. And to make an end is to make a beginning." It's a misquote, but it's clear what she's hoping to convey. It reminds me of another Eliot quote, one I cannot remember word for word—much like so many quotes I love and wish I could recall, not unlike those poems I want to learn by heart. The quote is something about stagnating in the late stages of life, about how we don't grow old but rather find ourselves standing still.

"You can freeze butter, right?" my wife asks, continuing to clean out the refrigerator.

"I assume so. Not sure."

There had been a surplus over the holidays. Now, with the celebrations behind us, we don't plan to use much butter. But, if butter is immune to freezer burn and can be frozen to stand still in time, maybe we can return to it, drop some of it in a sauté pan when we again have something to celebrate.

I return to the news.

Three people are dead in a truck accident in Indiana. The rig's driver was distracted placing his coffee in the cup holder and didn't realize traffic in front of him had slowed. Eight mangled vehicles, and more than a dozen people in hospitals. The dead never knew what happened. This, and the rest of it, takes me away from my original morning plan. I had been considering pushups. There have been several weeks without, despite my vague commitment to continue with them most days. Exercise seems so silly now as I think of the dead who never expected it. *Do we ever expect it?* My father did not. He wouldn't accept it, but aggressive cancer and daily hospice care rarely lead to anything good. It was the same for my mother. She didn't know. Her dementia was too far along. I knew it was coming. The doctors did, too. Both my father and mother were too young to die when we recognize how long people live these days.

One of the dead in the truck accident was only 19 years old.

The ancestry research I've been working through shows some hope for me. Even though my father and mother died in their late seventies, there are a few relatives who lived until their late eighties and early nineties. Working men and women, laborers, mostly. A great-grandfather made wooden barrels by hand for Iron City Brewing. And there was the great-great-grandfather — mentioned again in the documents — the coachman on the Isle of Wight who worked with horses in stables every day.

Last evening, I spoke with my younger son by phone. He was excited to tell me about his plans for putting down new hardwood in his kitchen, which would involve my help, of course. I wasn't as excited as he was, telling him it was a lot of work, and I didn't have a great deal of time in the next few weeks. Certainly, I would help, but I didn't express this so well. Now, I want to take it all back. My father helped me. There was the big backyard swing set for the kids. He built a pine cabinet I still own. And he was not such a young man when he measured wood and hammered nails to build a cedar deck on the back of my first real house. His skills were more finely honed than mine are today, as he was a carpenter by trade, building homes as a young father. Still, some of those abilities have been passed on, a meager amount, and yes, I too, like him, will help my son. If I carry my father's genes, I just may be dead in 15 years. Or tomorrow a semi-truck could mow me down. Maybe, somewhere in the DNA, the longevity gene made its way to me, but I can't count on it.

There are some do-it-yourself videos on the web, tutorials on removing vinyl flooring and replacing it with treated hardwood. I attend to my schedule and my calendar suggests a few open Sundays in the coming weeks. Then, I drop to the floor.

Uncertain I can pull off 20, I take a long deep breath, and tell myself I have no other choice. Through the final three, through the moans and burning forearms, blood rushes to my head and I am unmistakably resurrected, alive, convinced I have never appreciated pushups this much before.

# 22

It is the tooth. No, it's the jaw. A dull ache persists. Not necessarily a toothache; more like a muscle strain. Sometimes it pulsates, a quick burst of pain and then gone. A dentist appointment is scheduled in a week or so, but I am still unsure this has anything to do with a tooth. Old man aches and pains.

Tea is the drink. Moroccan tea—a gift to my wife from my son from a shop in southern Spain—is soothing. The aroma is vanilla. I sip in a quiet house and draw a sketch in my journal of a desert landscape—mountains, birds, sun, dry brush, and cacti. I'm planning to catch a train to the city at just after 6 a.m.

It was another anxious dream last night. I have many such dreams. In this one, I had forgotten about several important appointments, never attending any of them. I awoke believing for a moment that it was all true, and panicked. Overall, I've been sleeping reasonably well, but these dreams—mild nightmares of being late, forgetting a promise, or visions of being in a broadcast studio and unable to operate anything—are consistent. Have been for years. It seems now, however, that I remember them more often.

In my journal are those three poems I've promised myself to learn by heart. I haven't yet started to process them and a level of guilt creeps in. *Now is the time*, I say to myself. *Read them*, I tell myself. But I don't.

This is misplaced commitment. Too many balls in the air—teaching, writing, family promises, books to promote, appearances at workshops and author events. None of this is overwhelming, but this morning I want to turn all of it off. Flick the toggle. Something simpler is my hope, but I'm unsure what "simpler" means. Later today, I go to the city to begin production of an audiobook. I look forward to it but would like for it to be over as soon as possible. Is this what happens as you get older? Do you long for less? Less stuff. Fewer obligations. Do you instinctively crave time to be on your side, although it certainly is not? This is not about retirement, that traditional, melancholy malaise we have come to believe is good for us, somehow strangely cherished, and desired. No. It is more. It is about claiming what remains.

Light is opening the day outside, the light of a common day. *I think that's a lyric from a David Crosby song.* Through the kitchen window I look east beyond the trees; tints of blue lift from the horizon. The achy jaw has improved a bit. The morning dream-fueled anxiety has faded, as it mostly does, and in my journal, I sketch one more bird in flight over the mountain, and head for the train.

# 23

She is so patient, no pulling away or resistance. The brush rolls across her back and under her snout, along the rough spots behind the ears where the tangles tend to form. She is accepting all of it. Using scissors from the kitchen drawer, I trim the hair around her eyes and notice, once again, the white sclera. She rolls on her back and shows her belly. The dog needs some sprucing up before we travel to Galena, Illinois—a two-and-a-half-hour drive—and she's taken to my ex-wife's house for a sleepover, a one-night stay while I speak at a literary festival.

The dog will be 4 years old this summer, a young adult in dog years. But despite her relative maturity, she still dislikes being alone. In that way, she is an unhappy child when Mother drops her off at the sitter's home. This is not unusual, really. Loneliness worries all of us. Not solitude, that's a different existence. It is being alone that is unnerving. I have a friend who openly speaks of his worry of being alone in old age, alone emotionally. This seldom crosses my mind, despite considering the loneliness the dog must be anticipating. Maybe I should think about it more. What would being alone, truly alone, be like? The children gone on their own, my wife gone, my dog gone. It triggers a level of melancholy, but it does no good to contemplate what might be. The poets and the sages encourage us to live in the here and now, to hold tight to the present. But we all know it is not that easy.

Dental work was done earlier this week and the jaw is improving. The pain turned out to be a tooth, not a muscle. A return to the dentist's chair comes next week. Today there is a slight ache and I rub my chin. It is a process, I'm told. Old teeth are not fun. With the dog on her back, and her paws in the air,

I look at her teeth. The vet says to examine her gums now and then. They should be pinkish. They are. I think about flossing.

The sump pump line froze yesterday, and I look out the back door to the hose in the yard to be certain the mechanism is working. Ice has formed near the mouth of the line. That is a good sign, a suggestion that water has been exiting the hose, as it should. The weather has been brutal, frigid, and apocalyptic. The shed might take a long time to warm up this morning. The remote switch for the space heater is on, but there is little faith in what it can do when the thermometer on my phone reads well below freezing. Still, I reheat what is left of the black coffee and decide to wait it out. My bare feet are cold against the hardwood of the kitchen floor, and I search for slippers. One is by the gray chair in the living room; the other is lost somewhere. The dog often carries a slipper to other places in the house to sit with it and hold it in her mouth. Veterinarians say she does this to keep me close, anxious that I might leave her, troubled by the possibility of aloneness. The slipper is not near the stairs and not in the bathroom; nothing in the bedroom or under the dining-room table. It turns up in her dog bed next to an old tennis ball.

Before long, we will begin the drive to the festival, but standing next to the dog bed, I decide to bring the one slipper along in the car for the dog to have near her during the overnight stay. She is going to need it more than I will. Some of us are like that.

# 24

There is a sparkle in the air. On the tree-lined road, the January trees are wrapped in silvery ice, the mid-afternoon sun not warm enough to uncover the naked branches. Instead, the refracted light glints off the frozen limbs and shimmers across the sky. This will not last. The weather will change, and this scene will vanish. What is beautiful now will not be here tomorrow.

My wife and I are a few miles from the hotel where the literary festival will be held, and I am thinking about what has not been done. I am prepared enough for my talk—books packed in the trunk, pens for signing. But it is music that is on my mind, the songs I have not written. Songs I have not sung. The ice on the trees has captured me, yet there is distance between nature's allure and these thoughts, a deep chasm. What will you say to yourself when the days are at an end, and what you wanted to see, feel, or sing never was? Time is not always, and most importantly it is not forever. The ice on the trees is only for a moment. The music in my head will not always be there. I don't play enough anymore. My guitar sits idle too often. There are songs in me that I cannot hear, lost in the clutter. I write my words and hope for connections, the reason for this weekend at the literary festival. But now with the ice before me, I think of what will melt away before there is the chance to capture it.

# 25

The word is mead. M-e-a-d. It is discovered while working the crossword puzzle, the mini, from the *New York Times* in the early afternoon. The clue asks to name an ancient alcoholic drink that has made a twenty-first-century comeback. I'm not on the cutting edge of renaissance booze currently served to hipsters, so it takes some time to figure this out. That clue and the mysterious answer keep me from beating my best score—1:13. This was accomplished the other day. It was blazing speed for me. But there are many others who have worked the mini, people older than me that have completed the puzzle in seconds. I am hopelessly mediocre, a crossword imposter. Still, the crossword is done daily. It's believed these kinds of puzzles keep the brain from atrophy. I have no true evidence of this.

After the puzzle, I research more of my family history. Weeks ago, at the beginning of this discovery process, these names and photos and details flowed to me like a mountain river in spring. But now, what had been a nearly effortless digging around requires a full-on investigation. It is not as much fun when you must work at it. Maybe a break until the DNA analysis comes in the mail? Don't dwell on the past, they say, if you want to live a good life in your later years. But I dwell, anyway.

Last night, there was another dream of my sister. She often comes to me this way. And last night grief returned. Now in the daylight, I am again talking to the dead, rummaging through Ancestry.com, looking for messages from long ago. There are times when those long-gone souls reawaken. I am greedy of this time, more desirous of this stillness, even in dreams. So, at the kitchen counter, after running the snow blower over the driveway and walkway to the front stoop, doing what needs to be done in the present world, I am more certain than ever that talking to the dead, those souls now looking over my shoulder, is a privilege. It is not dwelling on the past, as some might say. Rather, it is the discovery of the future. DNA is alive. It travels in the blood, through the years, beyond us. It is not what has been; it is what will be. And so, I am astonished, and to be astonished "is one of the surest ways of not growing old too quickly," the words of Collette when she was elected to the Belgian Academy.

Yesterday, I played the guitar for over an hour, a triggered response after the trip to the literary festival. The guitar, a dinged-up Yamaha bought with saved-up cash from a newspaper route at the age of 16, sits quiet again, leaning against the wall. It is old, but it is new every time it is played. Like the dead found in the ancestry research, the guitar lives again when rediscovered.

A dental appointment waits. A college faculty meeting is set for this evening. But late tonight, as more anticipated snow falls across the window, I promise to pluck away and be astonished.

## 26

My son is here from Seattle for the thirtieth birthday party of my stepdaughter. Last night was filled with games at a funky bar in the city—a bar with a life-size Jenga set and a tire swing. After a late breakfast—scrambled eggs and pancakes—he borrows my car to meet an old friend in Lincoln Park, and I step off for a walk with the dog. Temperatures float around the freezing mark with a low-hung sky, the kind of day for which heavy wool blankets are made, and the icy leftover snow is crunchy to step on. At the turn in the street, a big black Land Rover is parked in a driveway. I had one of those once. It was great to drive, but lousy to maintain. The car my son is driving today is my old Nissan, a serviceable vehicle. But now I long for something different. When I told my son this, he asked, "Why?" "Sometimes you just want a new coat," I answered. A used Austin Mini had been on my mind, and my son scowled and laughed. The Minis are classic—especially the ones from the 1970s, black and boxy—but I don't have the energy or the money to buy one and maintain it properly. My son agreed with my **assessment** of the older models, at some level, but then in describing the newer ones he used the word "lame." In America the automobile is a symbol of the self, an accessory that says something about what's important or relevant to the owner. The old Nissan no longer does this for me; maybe it never did. Still, in the end, the old car will be detailed, cleaned up, and tuned up. But the heart wants something different.

While walking the dog, I tick off in my head what the next days will bring—early to the airport tomorrow for my son's flight back to Seattle, first day of classes for the new term at the college, and another dental appointment, a few more before this tooth work is completed. Unlike the car, the dental work is a necessity. Still, I'm sick of it. You get older and choices are made for you. There is more personal power to decide, yet your life, your body, and your heart ultimately make up your mind for you before there is opportunity or the energy to consider much else.

The dog steps lightly in some icy snow and pees.

There is one other item on the calendar—a fasting day. My wife and I are working through nearly a month of body cleansing, although that may be too strong a word. It is more of a reset—healthier foods, lots of water, some intermittent fasting. Tomorrow is a full day of no food. Water, coffee, and broth are permitted, but nothing else. I've done this before to rebalance, but my wife has not participated, and she will admit she is nervous. Keeping busy is the key. This is a choice, of course, a vow. It is not a materialistic rebranding of myself like a new car might suggest, or a medical inevitability like the dental work. This is a promise. Still, you don't truly understand a promise's weight until it is broken. The impact is only clear when it has been discarded. How many promises—small and big—have I rejected, tossed away? Promises forgotten. Promises I'm still trying to honor. Counting them in a lifetime would be impossible. Remembering them would be unreasonable. Yet, for those to whom a promise has been broken, they would undoubtedly remember. They might remind me. Or worse, they might *never* remind me and instead hold it forever inside. Tomorrow comes a promise, a commitment to fasting, but instead I think of a lifetime of kept and marred agreements. Age gives one the opportunity for this experience. Only the accumulation of years gives one the right.

Inside the house, I hang up my barn jacket in the closet and recall my wife's suggestion last night as we left for dinner that a new coat might be in order, a *real* coat. Something gray and nicer, she suggested. *Just like the car*, I think now. I love my old coat. I love the old Austin Minis. My favorite Timberland boots are showing wear, the soles nearly rubbed smooth, but I love them, too. There's that favorite belt fraying at the buckle, and a leather notebook darkened by more than a decade of oil from holding and carrying it in my hands. Like all the uncountable promises made and broken, these things, too, are eventually measured by how long we keep them close.

# 27

The late-afternoon light hangs in the air as if refusing to disperse, the world appearing to say, *move along, there's nothing to see here.* The drive from the city after a day at the college comes under a deep gray born from a tumbling sun filtered by clouds. To the west, the day tries to hold on, and to the east—the road behind and the horizon above are nearly black except for headlamps following me. The last light in the final minutes of the last hour always vanishes the swiftest.

The faces of people are all around. They fill the space in the traffic, coming to you without warning, reminding you of faces not seen in a long time. An old friend is now a grandfather, the evidence in a photo sent by text to me by another friend. Why we haven't been in touch is complicated. My sister's face comes to me, too. I see my father laughing and recall my mother's tired eyes as she rests in the bed at the nursing home. A friend from my hometown is distant in every way, but I see him in my mind's eye, and somehow believe that if I telephoned right now, he or his wife would answer as if no time had passed. I'm overdue on connecting with my aging aunt, and a cousin—a relative who may be a lost cause for a reconnection after so long. Smaller and smaller, the circle gets. These thoughts and faces appear now as the present days are getting longer, and the light is lasting. The space narrows but the daylight widens, measured but effortless change. I consider the radio but instead take in the muted whine and drone of the moving cars, a white noise that, for now, is a fitting soundtrack. It's not sadness or regret that surrounds, but acceptance of time gone by and the waning light of a single winter day that when separated from the season is no longer than the day before.

The fasting continues. No food since yesterday. Just black coffee, bone broth, and water. I never drink enough water. I've done well all day, but now, in between the remembering and the light, I imagine a big bowl of cereal covered with blueberries and bananas. It's not a craving, but instead a vision, like a spirit that comes to you when you're sleeping, one with no obvious message but simply appearing and standing silently before you as if you are supposed to know why they have made themselves visible. Before going home, there's yet another dental appointment to keep. It is to be quick—medicine for a crown to come later—and this visit, with good fortune, will keep my mind, for a time, away from food visions. *Stay busy. Don't think about what you are missing, what you have been denied. Think about what you can do right now instead.* Turning these thoughts into something philosophical is tempting, considering this drive in a fading day, visions of denied sustenance mixing with the remembrances of people in my past. But not everything has to have deep, significant meaning and weight. Sometimes hunger pangs are simply hunger pangs, and the hours of a day do not truly change despite the season, despite the effort to save time, and the sun will continue to rise and set for billions of days.

# 28

In class today, a student told the story of how she had once been exorcised. As a child, the grandmother—believed by many in her Mexican village to be a medium, a bridge between the living and dead—summoned an ancient Brazilian chief. The student said during the beckoning, the grandmother's eyes rolled back in her head and her voice dropped several octaves, while offering mystical guidance to members of her gathered family. The old woman then pointed to the child—now my student— and proclaimed, "This one is not well." Religious elders were summoned, and an exorcism was performed to purge the little girl's soul of evil.

"What was that like?" I asked.

"I don't remember all of it," my student said, "but I do remember the fear. It was terrifying."

"And those bad spirits? Were they no longer there?"

"I guess they are gone. But I never knew they were there in the first place, if they were at all."

This intense ritual forced upon a little girl is unimaginable. Yet, the faith in an otherworldly dynamic must have been incredibly powerful to warrant believers to permit it, even demand it, this involuntary alteration of one for the good of many.

It is hours after the class—the chair rolled back from the desk and my feet propped up. The overhead fluorescent lights are off, and the desk lamp is on. The door is open a crack and I hear students at the department reception desk in the foyer talking about the Grammy Awards, which had aired on television a few nights ago. "Music has changed so much," one says. "I wasn't sure who some of those nominated even were," another says. Change is unavoidable, but I am surprised the students did not identify with the musical change. I understand *my* ignorance, but theirs?

*Everything changes. What an obvious thought,* I say to myself. It is a contemplative mood I am in. Change is every day. My beard is grayer. My eyesight worsens and it is the norm to wear cheaters more often to read menus. Scratching the itch in between my shoulder blades is nearly impossible without standing with my back to a doorjamb and squirming to find the spot that needs attention. A year or two ago, reaching that spot with my hand was not so difficult. These changes are not forced upon me. They simply occur, falling into place within the process of time. An exorcism, one might say, is a fortified change, like a coup, a hostile takeover for what is believed to be a better good; it is not only for the exorcised, but for society, family, and the world. My changes are without debate, but they are not linked to some greater good, and they will transpire no matter my state of mind. There remains the capacity to embrace or reject them. Accept or fight.

There is a voice on the other side of the door.

"All music is still only about one thing, when it comes down to it," the student says, once again referring to the music awards. "Then and now and always, it will be about love. That, no matter what, is never going to change."

*Yes,* I say to myself. *That is true.* But the kind of love, the person we love, how and when we fall in or out of love, change all the time. One must be reckless when it comes to affairs of the heart. Fall in love with life. Be zealous, no matter how vulnerable it makes you. Allow the heart to be open. Only with this belief, and a pledge to a passionate life, comes true change. In this, change is good, natural, free from resistance. *Have I been reckless with love in all my years?*

A romantic, I have been called, a description that conjures up a cliché. Instead, I would rather consider myself a contemplative. Not in the sense of religion or spiritualism, for a contemplative life is not defined by a certain level of practice or belief. This approach to life is more about pushing beyond the common to the genuine. It might mean melding this ideal with a meditative life of self-awareness, maybe the practice of yoga, for instance, but it also may not. Yoga has not delivered to me what others have discovered, although meditating in both the traditional way and by simply closing my eyes for a time on a commuter train or park bench have at times worked. In these processes, these contemplations, I have ultimately sought change, both tiny increments and big shifts. In all cases—in love, in meditation, in teaching, in writing, in walking a woodland trail, in a celebratory dinner, in music—it has been an attempt at metamorphosis and imagination. "The unexamined life is not worth living," Socrates is reported to have said. He was condemned for his wisdom, yes, but he also insisted he would rather die than not be able to ask questions of his life and the lives around him, leading to a world without curiosity, a world in which he did not want to exist. What comes with examination? Change. To simply assess or scrutinize is only one side of the equation. Sometimes, like an exorcism forced on that child, examination comes without fully being aware, demandingly, and powerfully. In other ways, it comes innately, naturally. Shifting oneself, incrementally or dramatically by one's own power or by another force toward a more genuine state, is the essence of the art of living.

Walking to my car in the parking lot, I notice tall construction boards erected around the outside of one of the campus buildings. They conceal the large street-level windows and the outer façade. Behind them I hear the strike of a hammer and the buzz of an electrical saw, and unidentifiable voices. Change is coming, an update, a reconstruction someone wanted, maybe demanded, maybe simply needed. If the building could talk, would it care to complain? Did it want these changes? Did it accept them, or does it protest? The stately stone building has stood for decades, the same as it was constructed since the 1940s.

This would make it 80 years of age—an old man who just wants to be left alone. Still, change is happening no matter how the building feels—if it could—or what it wants—if it knew. Now it is a matter of acceptance and a decision—for me, or for this personified building—to either embrace the change or struggle to push it away.

# 29

At first glance, it appears Donna is missing. The fishbowl, with the water and the light catching it, sometimes acts as a prism, making it difficult to see inside. After looking left and right and then straight down from the top, Donna is found, close to the surface at the back of the bowl.

Any day now Donna will be dead. She's lived beyond probabilities. Some weeks ago, I asked aloud about the life expectancy of a guppy. A Google search suggested a maximum of two years. Time is close.

Donna was purchased just over two years ago in an impromptu trip to the pet store with my grown stepdaughter. So, in guppy terms, Donna is quite elderly. Maybe in hospice care at this point. But at this moment at least, Donna's gills are continuing to function.

*Are her eyes buggier than yesterday? Is she moving more slowly?* I drop in a sliver of fish food. *Why is she not eating it? She sees it, doesn't she?*

One morning poor Donna will be found floating. But today, she lives.

# 30

It's Super Bowl Sunday. 8:10 a.m. Neil Young whines from the smart speaker: "Old man, take a look at my life." Young was 24 when he wrote that song. He proclaims it in the lyrics. As the story goes, Young wrote the words about the old caretaker at his ranch who, as Young once put it, "came with the place." Before I knew that bit of musical history, I had chided young Neil for singing about the challenges of old age when he had spent only two decades on earth. Now, on this morning, I think differently.

My wife and I will watch football with my son and his wife, another couple, and my ex-wife at her home a few miles from us. Not much skin in the game today, which permits one, as my son has said, to simply enjoy football. Sometimes it is more fun to watch when you are viewing it as a game and not through the gauze of passion or pride in a favorite team. The spread online at the ESPN site shows the Chiefs favored by two points over San Francisco. That's a statistical wash. The website is loaded with Super Bowl stories, including the one on the 49ers' quarterback. He grew up just outside Chicago. I reject falling into the hometown hero vortex, holding to the idea of watching the game for the sake of the game. Switching gears, I search my email to double-check airline reservations and then a weather site to see the coming temperatures in Arizona. The golf trip with my stepson is a few days away. Looks like it will be a day of mild temperatures and sunshine. Through the living-room window, I see a dusting of snow left on the sidewalk from overnight.

Neil is still singing. It is the line about not "getting lost."

Everything gets lost. Where are my keys? I swear I put my wallet *right here*. The confirmation email for the trip's accommodation is hiding in the mess of other emails. This is the unassuming forgetfulness that comes with age that you pray will not worsen. Still, you know it will. You'll lose a cherished photograph, then a memory, and then a friend. Neil got that part right. Later today, someone will lose the big game. Careers shaken and shifted. And there will be good and bad memories for the fans and for those of us watching from far away. But in time, much will be forgotten or at least muted enough to go forever out of focus. Sure, there will be video to remind us, but that's not a memory. It is only the digital spark that might help us recall what was once real, moments that technology cannot truly recapture. When the last frame fades, the memory will begin its slide back to the dark corners of the mind.

In Neil's song, he reminds the old man that despite his age, he, too, was young once. Young is in his seventies now. The voice I hear this morning singing that recorded song is 50 years younger, and yet, there is wisdom. *What kind of wisdom did I possess at 24? Where was I then? What was I doing? Who was I at 24?* It takes some time to calculate the answers, and yet there is uncertainty if what is remembered is correct, or if the recollections now slowly coming into vague focus are only what remain of an old man's lost memory.

In the last year of my mother's life, there were times when she was not sure who I was. Sometimes when I visited the nursing home, she would sit up in her bed and speak with me as if I were my dead father, addressing me by his name. Other times she would ask, "Who are you, again?" Dementia came slowly, simple forgetfulness at first, misplacing her glasses, and then not recalling whether she had eaten breakfast. But it was when she began to lose the ability to identify people, to understand how they fit into her life or why they were in her room at all, that being with her became difficult to navigate. I wanted so much to be with her, but being physically there had become painful, a disorientation that was not only hers, but mine, too. My own struggle was hard to shake while witnessing my mother slowly lose her mind.

Busying your mind, they say, will help keep it young. Brain activity is like exercise for gray matter. As Neil's song fades out on its final chords, I find the *New York Times* mini crossword on my phone and get to work. Clue: Guiding principle. Starts with the letter T. Five letters. T-e-n-e-t. Clue: Petunia Dursley to Harry Potter. *Damn. Not a Harry Potter guy.* I will have to rely on other clues to fill in those empty spaces. Turns out, Petunia is Harry's aunt. Sometimes answers don't come easily, and the brain simply needs a little help.

# 31

The sky is deep red at the horizon. The layer above is blue and beyond that is the black of fallen night. And appearing to rise from the ground like a large hand missing two of its fingers is the silhouette of a cactus, a saguaro, the tree of the desert. Farther to the west, too far to see, is the wildlife reserve and beyond that are the Joshua trees. For the Natives, these are the trees of life, using their tough leaves to weave baskets and sandals, the tree buds and seeds for food. The early Mormons believed the Joshua branches—twisted like the imagined vegetation of Dr. Seuss—were pointing their people westward, guiding them to something better, just as the biblical figure, friend and assistant to Moses, was said to have done. And for me, sitting alone in the bubbling waters of a hot tub, far from the highway and city lights, with only the song of what I believe is a nightjar interrupting the silence, I wonder why this land so joyously welcomes me.

I am here to play golf, a long-awaited trip with my stepson. It was a full day today. Out in the sun and the desert foothills for nearly ten hours under a brilliant blue, cloudless sky. An eagle flew high above an endless stretch of sage, the sun illuminating the bird's white tail. Roadrunners zipped across our path. Desert chipmunks stole food from the golf cart. The game has brought me here, but it is the land that has taken my heart. This is not surprising. I've been here before—Arizona, the desert, Navajo Nation—and I've experienced similar connections to this arid land, red dirt, and the vastness. Still, I am unsure what fuels this.

The anticipated DNA test results will surely show most of what I have known: a family with much of its roots in the British Isles. Surely nothing that would genetically link me to the American Southwest. The Isle of Wight, where my English grandfather was born, is halfway around the world from the cactus I see in the distance. My maternal great-grandfather came from Ireland's east coast where rolling dunes protect the shores and the Hook Lighthouse has been guiding the sailor's way for nearly a thousand years. I am drawn to lighthouses, but who isn't? And windswept shorelines have been forever calling humans to their magnificence. So then, where does the American Southwest fit into the chromosomal puzzle, if at all?

The hot tub shuts off. For safety, it is on a timer. But I am not ready to leave. The temperature has dropped significantly in the last 30 minutes. I step out and the air bites my bare legs and the chill clings to my soaking black tee shirt like a leech. A twist of the knob on the tub's timer and the bubbles begin again. After quickly shaking water from my arms, believing it might warm me somehow, I'm back in, my neck resting against a corner ledge and looking west. The color along the horizon now is midnight blue, and high in the sky is a single star, vivid and still. It is the only light besides the full moon behind me to the east. That brightest light is not a star at all. It is Venus, a fact I had learned on other nights of stargazing. Venus is so intense tonight, the sunlight bouncing off the planet's clouds, that it fools me. For a moment it appears to be a plane. Mars is closer to the earth, but Venus is most luminous. It is the light that Native Americans called the Morning Star, as it remained brightest at dawn in ancient skies. The symbol of that star is one of hope and guidance. Not unlike the Joshua tree. Maybe this is what the relationship with this land is about—the hope and guidance it must give, trusting that a dream can become real, that an expectation or desire can be yours. The wish is to remember this evening, its undisturbed beauty. The hope, however, is that what has been discovered tonight lasts for many days, however many or few that may be.

The tub's timer clicks off again, and I realize I have forgotten to bring a towel. My shorts are dripping; and like before, the black tee shirt sticks hard to my shoulders and chest. Slipping on my shoes, I grumble. *Jesus, it's cold.* And then for a fleeting moment, I think of Scotland and the bookstore I didn't buy and the other that allows one to run it while living in the upstairs apartment. *It can be bitterly cold in Scotland. But it, too, is gorgeous country, gorgeous like tonight. Maybe the DNA test will show a bit of Scotland in my blood.*

Back at the condominium, the closest I can get to the possibility of that heritage is inside a glass of whisky on ice.

# 32

The sun gleams off the snow that fell the day before, bright light breaking through the kitchen window. The days just ahead of Valentine's Day are so often like this—frigid but shining, one more period of harshness before we lean into a new season. We hang our hopes on a relatively mild afternoon, or damp ground where inches of snow had once been, or a few more seconds of light added to the day.

Engrossed in a *New York Times* article—a piece from the previous Sunday's magazine section—I am only half-hearing my wife's comments on what she is reading about Pete Buttigieg, the former mayor of South Bend. A profile of the German artist Anselm Kiefer written by Karl Ove Knausgaard is more compelling at the moment. His words seep into me; they are under my skin. Not only has Knausgaard's style—no pretense, only superior observation—taken hold, but Kiefer's artistic life, a combination of unsettling privilege and stunning creative sensitivity, captivates me. He is an old man, Kiefer is. Seventy-one, Knausgaard writes. But he doesn't look 71, observes the writer. *Do I look 63?* Kiefer's life angers me, but I'm drawn to it. He visits friends in castles for wine and dinner, places where others are forbidden or simply cannot go. He travels regularly by helicopter. Is this what an artist has become in the twenty-first century?

The sharp cold and brilliant sun of the February day hold within them my current mood—bitter but illuminated, disheartened but hopeful. The world is frozen. It is dead. Cryogenically stopped in time. Put in storage. It waits for its new cue. I think of the tulip bulbs I planted last fall. *Did the squirrels get to them before the ground became impossible to crack? Will the flowers make it? Will they die?* Death. It is the ultimate mystery. *Who is it that gets to discover the answers?* We assume it is the old who will find out first, like Kiefer, the artist. He, like all renowned artists, has the level of insight to help reveal the answers when his time has run out. At least this is what many believe. How we live will determine if we see heaven, if we know the afterlife, if there is something else. Yet religions offer this only to keep us in check. What about the child who dies and has no time to prove their ultimate worth to the gods? And what about people like the 71-year-old Kiefer who, for some, may be grabbing far too much opportunity for the life he has chosen, as if somehow one does not deserve the other. Will he be privileged with the answer? The only answer for any of us is tied directly to the act that most of us do not wish to experience.

I should shovel some of the walkway but will not. It is too cold, and it is comfortable where I sit. Death is out there, even though it is draped in sunshine. Life, however, is inside, and I choose that for now. Whether or not I am living what remains of my time as I should, I do not know. Am I pleasing the gods? I'll leave that to higher judgment. And that is all Kiefer can do. All Knausgaard can do. All any of us can do.

# 33

A soft light enters through the white blinds on the east-facing window as I pull away the comforter and the sheets. Bed comes early tonight. There is radio work in the morning, my scheduled Saturday broadcasts, which I have conducted for many years. The journalist side of my world. None of this is unusual. But there is this light in the room, muted like the strokes in a watercolor, dusty like the light one might find falling through the window at dawn in an old cabin in the woods. The fallen sun is gone but it will come again tomorrow, and more than ever, it seems, this is certain. It is clearer than ever tonight that the coming and closing of a day is not only the world's timepiece; it is, as Dylan Thomas wrote, "the heaven between the stars." It is the unknown amid the concrete and intangible, and Heaven, like time—real or imagined, manmade or of the natural world— is a mystery.

My wife and I watched the movie *Set Fire to the Stars* on Netflix tonight, the story of Dylan Thomas' first visit to America and the relationship with his tour manager, the academic John Malcolm Brinnin, a friendship that opened the eyes of both men to the artistic life, authenticity, and the reality that all any of us have is what is in front of us. Time backward is just that. Gone. Time forward is still ours. The light in the window tonight is a reminder.

With my head on the pillow, I look to the ceiling. In the time that remains for me, what is it that I want to do? I want to write. Life without the kind of examination that writing brings would not be worth it. I want to love. My wife and my children are my flowers. I want to walk in the woods. There's that bookstore in Scotland. There's the pull of the desert. And any day now, the analysis will arrive, the detailed DNA particulars. When I was young, matters of ancestry were only of marginal interest, a story or a memory's laugh recalled at a holiday family gathering. Now they are nothing less than necessity. The yank of the past pulls far more vigorously. What will the results reveal? Maybe it will be simple confirmation. But confirmation is also powerful. What will happen next? Travel to ancestral lands? More familial detective work? This, too, is part of what I want to do with the time left.

It is difficult to close my eyes. *Mysteries*, I tell myself, *are incredibly alluring*. Rolling to one side, I bury my face in the pillow. Comfort, despite my hiding, stays with me. Despite all the questions, there is no urgency for answers. The questions are beautiful enough for now. Sleep takes time tonight, but dreams come quickly.

# 34

Needed updates to the will are overdue. They are close to being ready, yet I am slow to sign off on all of it, a battle between the head and the heart. An update is just what is needed, wholeheartedly, but a self-imposed urgency to finish the work brings me face to face with the inevitable. It is not death that unsettles, for death always surrounds the production of a last will and testament, the anticipation of signing one's name on the dotted line. Instead, it is how death demands that you do this.

There are the names, my sons' and my wife's. There are the addresses and the phone numbers. The social security numbers and the percentages of the money saved, 33% of a life. I fill in the spaces, write my name on the space highlighted by the financial advisor with a yellow marker. And on my computer, I write more words, an addendum. Who gets the guitars; who gets my father's onyx ring, the one my mother gave him at their wedding? Who takes possession of my mother's wedding ring? Cremation? Burial? Decomposition in the wilds of Oregon? Ashes to dirt. Some of these questions I am able to answer, others not so sure. Not yet. My wife says these documents need to be notarized. Apparently, my wishes are not really mine until the lawyers say so.

My parents had no money. There was no inheritance. Their home was sold to my sister before my mother's dementia. She lived there after their deaths. Then the alcohol took over. She rented rooms to people she didn't know. Everything fell apart. The home I grew up in was sold at a sheriff's sale. My sister had no money, nothing of any worth or significance to pass along. She had sold or lost everything. Once, when she was sober, she told me that she wanted to be cremated, scattered in her favorite places. There was no belief in God and no need for funerals and ceremony. Her ashes are on mountains, inside Heinz Field — the home of her beloved Steelers — and in the ground near the graves of our parents, overlooking a hill of maples. My sister had no will, no formal documents of any kind, but she knew what she wanted in death more than what she wanted in life. She wasn't permitted to age, but the loss was not her death. The loss was what died inside her while she lived.

I close the computer, having enough of death for now, enough preparation for what becomes everyone's fate. Death will find us all. For now, I choose this good home around me, the music that plays from the speaker, the poetry in the book on the side table. There's a dog beside me, holding my watch cap in her mouth, nuzzling it close. She glances at me, reassured that I will stay put. And at the kitchen counter is my wife, her back to me, reading the newspaper the old-fashioned way. Coffee nearby. Content. Which one of us will go first? Who will be left behind? Who will remain when the other disappears? When life fractures, poetry arises, someone once said or wrote. There are always pieces of each of us left along the long trail, helping others to put together what has been shattered. Memories in the right places, like ointment for a wound, eventually leave behind little scars that prove we have lived.

# 35

The girl on the bus is waving. She has brown hair and big eyes, but the tall seat obscures her mouth, and I cannot see her full expression. The wave is vigorous, yet shy; she lifts her hand just slightly above her head. When I smile and return the wave, she ducks behind the seat and out of sight. After several you-see-me-then-you-don't games, her friend joins her, a blonde girl about the same age, maybe 7 years old. She, too, waves and hides. Then they do it together, wave and when I wave back, they vanish, an exchange that has me smiling as I sit in my car just behind the yellow school bus, inching along on a highway into the city. Innocence is not gone; it is only harder to notice.

Many years before, my family—my mother, father, sister, and I—rode north toward Lake Erie on a summer day. Traffic was tight; the car next to us surged ahead then slowed and nearly stopped, over and over for what seemed like forever, our car doing the same. From my seat I saw a little boy, about the same age as me, I presumed, sitting in the back seat of the other auto. Our eyes met for a moment, and I raised my hand to wave. The boy turned away. But I kept watching, waiting for him to look again. For a long time, the two cars crept along together through the heavy traffic, side by side, but the boy never returned to the window.

It is odd what we remember and what we forget. Recalling my sons' birthday parties some 20 years ago is so easy, but I cannot remember what I did on my own birthday last November. I clearly recall my father with tears in his eyes telling me he loved me the night before I moved away from my hometown for good. A memory of my mother standing in her kitchen is clear, white flour dust on her Christmas apron, offering this little boy what she called a snowball cookie, made with sticky dough, nuts, and lots of sugar. And I can see the eyes of a woman I had just met, the woman who would in time become my wife, widen, and sparkle when over our first coffee date, we shared our love of music. There are many beautiful moments that have been lost in time—smiles and kisses and hugs and tears that are gone for good. Why remember the boy in the car so many years ago, the one who didn't return the wave? There are those who say we remember only what serves us, what we can use later to understand ourselves—the good and the bad, what gives us joy and what cuts deep. Maybe then, in aging, we refine those memories, sifting through the past to permit only the recollections that shape us into who we always should have been.

The girls on the bus, the ones waving and hiding, the ones I now see giggling in a silly exchange, will they remember this moment many years from now? Will they someday recall the man in the car behind their school bus, who waved back again and again, who smiled at them, and who now, like them, giggles, too?

The bus takes the next exit and heads north, across the road above the highway and out of sight.

# 36

Four poems—specific parts of them, certain stanzas, and lines—
these are the poems I have vowed to memorize, words that have
seeped into me. It took some time to decide on which lines to
work on, although I had many ideas and much time to consider
them and confirm. I am far from a poetry scholar and know
little of what is truly brilliant here, other than what the more
literary have highlighted. I do know, however, what poetry is
capable of doing to your heart.

Leaves whip in circles above the sidewalk like little tornadoes,
visible through the tall windows in the corner of a coffee shop
on an afternoon that despite its February personality is singing
of May sunshine. Sunglasses were needed to arrive here and,
even while sitting inside, sunglasses rest on my nose. Before me
is my notebook, and it is here that I begin to write the words
of Auden, Yeats, and Dylan Thomas. If I copy them here, it will
help me begin to keep them close, reserve them to memory, and
eventually allow me to recite them at will.

Auden is first. The stanza is from "As I Walked Out One
Evening." My belief, like others more perceptive, is that this
poem is about how Time is impossible to control, that it has the
upper hand. "You cannot conquer time," Auden wrote. This is
obvious, maybe. But the poem's depth is linked to something
deeper, how love endures. The words were originally written
for music, a literary ballad, and this confirms the purpose of the
poem's rhythm.

Yeats is next. He writes of the pilgrim's soul, a description
that has always fascinated, but the meaning eludes me. It has
been interpreted in many ways. For me, however, that phrase
represents a traveler, a searcher. "When You Are Old" contains
some of the most beautiful lines in poetry. How can you not

cherish a poem about how love will always remain no matter how age weathers us? I write down the last line of the second stanza: "And loved the sorrows of your changing face."

And now, to Thomas. I struggle with two stanzas that I love but I am drawn to one line over and over: "Time held me green and dying." "Fern Hill" is Thomas' look back at his childhood, and the splendid days on his aunt's farm in Wales. Throughout the poem he explores the passage of Time, including asking his reader to investigate their own past, present, future days, and to discover how the child still lives in them despite the years. You may be young, but even then, you are forever dying. Still, it is not meant to be a sad truth. Instead, it is to remind us that childhood happiness can always be, even as Time chisels away, if only we will continue to summon it. This is not a scholar's skilled analysis or Thomas' explanation; it is mine.

There are children walking home from school now. Girls wearing big fluffy boots and dressed in plaid skirts are traveling in pairs across the train tracks, their hair blowing across their laughing faces. Three boys, maybe from the same school, run from one end of the street to the other—one carries a hulking backpack, another is empty-handed, and the third has a skateboard under his arm. Once at the sidewalk, the skateboard boy throws his ride to the ground. I can hear the hard rubber wheels hit the cold pavement. He jumps aboard and pushes off with one foot, zipping beyond his friends. In his own world now, his buddies left behind, he appears to be singular and free. As he reaches the crosswalk, he encounters a pair of the skirted girls, flips his hoodie from his head, and says something to them I cannot hear. One of the girls throws back her head in laughter, and the boy smiles. With practiced ability, he then becomes momentarily airborne and flips the skateboard, skillfully returning to it and its forward motion. The young peacock unfurling his feathers. He will remember that girl's laughter for many days, and in many years at some other time and place, when there before him is yet another laughing girl, he will recall again this girl in the plaid skirt by the train tracks on a cold February day when he was young.

There is no coincidence why I have chosen these poems and these particular lines. They represent where I have been and where I am now, waiting for spring to appear in the slowly evolving light while the big candle burns. The boys and girls laugh, knowing nothing of what is to come in their worlds, innocent of what God is or was or will be, believing that one will always be skateboarding, always have the peacock unfurling before them, and unaware of inevitable broken dreams or of unending love, or of the beauty of crying without being told to stop, or understanding that the night's darkness is what revives the day, or of the wisdom of Christopher Robin or Calvin and Hobbes, or that the only real truth is found in moving forward.

The results came in an email. Details of lives linked. Centuries old. Lands far from here, yet close. A link is clicked, and it takes me to a chart. Percentages are revealed. Little boxes of ancestral presents, evidence of familial bloodlines, the blood in my own veins.

A pie chart is to the right of the website page. Wales and southern England, specifically the Isle of Wight, is highlighted in mustard color on the map to the left. The ethnicity estimation points directly to the small island off the southern coast and claims 41% is directly linked to this region. Welsh, too, it says. Not sure where or how that comes into play. The confirmation on my great-great-grandfather is before me. He was a coachman on the Isle, as the handed-down knowledge had claimed. And then there is County Wexford, Ireland, green on the map. This rural stretch is the land the Dugans called home, my paternal grandmother's side of the family. Another confirmation. More numbers: Germanic Europe 16%; Czech Republic, Poland, Lithuania 12%. My father's father was German. My mother's mother had a tiny bit of Polish in her genes. Confirmation. Then, something unexpected: Norway 2% and Spain 2%. I look again and read a link to the percentage markers:

The earliest inhabitants of the Norway region were strong, seafaring peoples.

And:

The heart of the region of Spain lies in the Iberian Peninsula, framed by the granite peaks and plunging falls of the Pyrenees on the French border in the north and sunny Mediterranean beaches in the south. This region has seen a long parade of invaders, including Celts, Romans, and Germanic Visigoths.

These are indirect links, circuitous relations to First Man. Not genetic links a century old, but ancient, primal fossils of human connections impossible to comprehend. Others who have proceeded with ancestral research have said that the single-digit percentages can mostly be dismissed, that they are not always reliable.

I google "The accuracy of DNA testing." There is a great deal about this, so many questions. So many companies and services. Some scientists dismiss the entire process; others see merit. Still others ride the fence. It is a wide brush, one article suggests. Grain of salt, another offers. Despite skepticism, I remain intrigued. Norway? Spain? *Wasn't southeastern Ireland once Viking country?* Who were these people? Generations later, centuries later, evidence of their existence is revealed. It is impossible not to link oneself to ancient worlds.

Navigating through the site, I find a link that allows you to create a poster and a photo book, the commercialization of my findings. I skip it. In another section of the site, there's an opportunity to upgrade to a health test, one that identifies markers of genetic risks. I skip it. They are only portals of DNA capitalism; DNA being sold back to me as a series of secrets to unveil as if being asked to choose a door on *The Price Is Right*. What is behind that curtain? For a few dollars more, you can find out.

There is a recent book about an author who through her own DNA test discovered her biological father. Reaching out to him was risky and carried with it unavoidable anxiety, but despite this, the two eventually met. Neither will ever be the same. No revelation of this level for me. Yet I, too, will never be the same, even though most of what has been discovered has been a series of validations. The question now is what to do with this knowledge, these mystical longings, these reawakened chromosomes. Under a modern medical microscope, chromosomes are invisible, but in the division process the DNA is visible. My results have shaken up this activity. My saliva sample has divided me into percentages of English horsemen, Irish maids, farmers, and seafarers. It has pointed to regions where ghosts have walked.

Another internet search finds images of the Isle of Wight, images of County Wexford—cottages and hills of green, the sea and the mountains. If I flew to London, I could take the train to southern England and then to the Isle, and a ferry to the town of Wexford. Laugharne, Wales—Dylan Thomas' town—might be only a car ride or train away. His boathouse, the place where he worked, sits near the estuary. *Would I confirm the Welsh in my blood?* My wife would come with me, I'm certain. But as quickly as the idea is considered, I dismiss it. It is selfish, an intimate parade for one to the past. Still, I save the links to several websites, type notes into a document, title it My Past, save it to my desktop, and wonder if this enthusiasm is only temporary, fueled by the newness of the findings.

On my phone is a grainy photo of Lawrence Dugan, my great-grandfather. It was saved after finding it on the ancestry site a few weeks ago, a photo new to me, a face I'd never seen. When my older son saw it, he gasped. The resemblance is striking. The shape of Lawrence's bald head, his eyes, even his thin lips are unmistakably mine. With the image before me now, I see him differently. It is not the visual that holds me. Instead, it is the evolutionary force, the reality that the blood of Lawrence Dugan is running through me—the soft hills of County Wexford, the breezes off the waters of Saint George's Channel and the Irish Sea, the Gaelic songs that roll out of the pubs. All of it comforts me like a familial quilt. What would I say to Lawrence Dugan if he were before me now, wearing his dark wool vest and carrying a pipe between his teeth, the way I see him in this photograph? I'm certain the words would come eventually, and we would laugh and tell stories.

There's an old Irish saying my grandmother would recall: *May the Good Lord take a liking to you—but not too soon.* Lawrence Dugan died on July 22, 1920, at the age of 63. My age. That's too soon, yes, but maybe the Good Lord liked Lawrence Dugan a whole hell of a lot.

# 38

Southwest Pennsylvania is a great steel beam that holds me true, arrow straight and unbendable. If you grow up in a steel town, you stand upright and proud. Not prideful, just undeniably certain of where you come from. No pretense. No Hollywood. Steel-town people have a hard-edged will, no gray in their truths. They will give you their very best if they know that you will do the same. If they are not deer hunters or bass fisherman, do not drink beer from long-neck bottles, or do not live and die by the sporting games grown men play, then they love someone who does. They prefer mountains to prairies, and rivers to oceans. They are raised in cold winters, and sticky summers, and beneath the ringing bells of churches where women wear hats and men wear ties, and little boys and girls hold out their hands and their tongues to take the holy wafer. Grandmothers live within walking distance. Fathers' garages hold treasures — odd nails, strange screws, and hammers with carved wooden handles. Mothers' kitchens never lose the aroma of coffee, a hot skillet, toasted bread, or salty broth. It is the America where the blue-collar man, the working class, was born. It doesn't matter if you never toiled in a mill; it only matters that the ones before you did, big men who bulged from their shirts, who celebrated with a shot and a beer, who inhaled smoky air and then demanded their industrialist bosses find a better way, the men who insisted that the steel they produced also produced durable men who could live to love their families for a long time. Those unbendable beams — the real and the ones constructed in men's souls — remain, holding up everything.

I think of my hometown's hold on me as I walk the dog on this first day of March. The month is coming in like a lamb — sunshine and a consistent light breeze out of the south.

Before the day is over it will be comfortably warm. My mother never missed noting the weather on March's first day, reminding my sister and me of the mysteries of March. If it came in like a lamb, she warned, it would go out like a lion, and spring would have to wait. It is the birth of March that finds me swimming in the past, thinking of steelworkers and sportsmen and shot-and-beer evenings and how I may not have carried on that tradition, yet it is deep inside me, tangled in the genes. The month of March and my mother's warning of how the season would unfold have awakened a latent but irrepressible part of me. In my steel town you buried money on New Year's Eve and cut a locket of hair on Good Friday for luck. You skipped school on opening day of the baseball season to go to Forbes Field to offer the Pirates the best chance of a great year. And on March 1st, you wished for the roughest weather possible so that it would be assured that spring would come fully alive in four weeks. Hope. That's what it was about. Hope for something better. Hope for a good life. If hope in a steel town was born out of working hard, choosing what was right, and praying on Sundays, then certainly wishing for an early spring in a month that could easily be unpredictably cruel was a good way to live.

All of it comes together on this first day of the month—the DNA test, the influence of family, faith, and steel, and today's sun through the naked trees, trees that will hopefully burst with buds in the coming weeks and reject the adage about the snarling seasonal lion. Walking in the day's quiet early hours, I am reminded that everything on my mind today will guide my tomorrow and all the days ahead, and the steel beams that hold me up, despite the rust, will remain indestructible, the rivets tight and strong, and I will look to what the end of March will bring.

# 39

The two of us face each other in a booth at a restaurant called Flappy's. It's a funny name and we joke about it, pronouncing it out loud to each other in absurd inflections. *Flapp-ee! Flap-pay!* Earlier I had helped my son nail trim around his new kitchen floor. It took longer than we had hoped. Now, he sips water and I drink coffee, and wait for a breakfast quesadilla for me and a chicken sandwich for him.

"I'm achy," I say.

"You should be," my son says. "After all, you're what? Eighty?" He laughs.

"Eighty?" I say. "I'll never make 80."

"Don't say that," he says, his face revealing mild panic.

I had been on the kitchen floor on my back and side, hammering finishing nails into quarter-round. There were awkward angles, on my knees and leaning on my elbows with a great deal of weight on my shoulders so that there was space and leverage to do the job.

"No one in my family has ever been 80," I say.

That is not true. My great aunt lived into her eighties and my great-grandfather on my dad's side lived to be 91. But my mother, father, sister, and grandparents on my mother's side never made it past 77. Two of them died in their fifties.

My son pauses and looks past me. In a few seconds, his eyes refocus and meet mine.

"How old are you really?"

"I'm 63. Be 64 this year."

My son appears to be counting in his head, matching his 27 years with mine. Maybe he is thinking of his future children, calculating their ages, his wife's, and his own against mine.

"2036," he says. "Is that right?"

"When I turn 80?"

I think for a moment and nod.

The waitress delivers our food. He asks for hot sauce. We eat in silence.

# 40

The hat looks better. Better than yesterday. Staring into the bathroom mirror, I tilt my head to the side and then the other. Yes, better. The manufacturer suggests it can be rolled up for travel, as it has been for several months. The clerk at the hat store would be appalled. It was purchased for a trip to Spain last summer. Hot summer days in Granada, one needs a hat, especially an old guy with a hairless head. The hat is made of raffia straw, lightweight, center dent, with a small brim. The trim around the crown is a dark leather braid. It had looked so good on the first day, but the rough storage warped it out of shape, and it needed to be massaged, dampened a bit, and massaged again. Care instructions on the hat maker's website suggested placing it upside down, so I did that, sitting it on top of the tall wooden buffet in the living room for a full day. And now, in the morning before the mirror, the hat is back on my head, looking better.

But this is not the original reason I am in the bathroom before the glass.

In a few minutes I'm off, yet again, to the dentist. Two crowns are waiting, steel and porcelain to replace old-man teeth. More work than first anticipated weeks ago. Looking in the mirror, I study my smile. I am blessed with straight teeth, and they remain in place like little soldiers. After the crowns, I might want to have some professional whitening done.

When I was young, the dentist filled cavities with metal and in time—I'm told—teeth shift when filled this way, the mouth changes, and cracks form in the enamel. It got bad in there. Couldn't save the teeth. Time and age do a number on a body. In my late thirties, I was told I needed to medicate hypertension. The family genes had caught up with me and it made me feel older than I was. My hair had already fallen out, leaving only memories of my shoulder-length, wavy, rock-n-roll locks. Every physical over the last many years has also included the check of the walnut in the urethra, and there is the yearly stress test. Wires attached with sticky probes all over my body as the tech urges me to run faster on the treadmill and devilishly inches up the incline every few minutes. I had a heart attack a few years ago at the same age that my father had his. Lucky, I was. Recovered well. It was not the same for my father, who had to undergo a quadruple bypass. For him, the stress tests were far less intense. Mine have been more so, and successful since the stent was put in. But we all know, someday that won't be the case. It is just the way it goes. I am old enough to have had two colonoscopies. Medicine has improved on the taste of the liquid you must drink, although the exit process is still unpleasant. I've made it through many of the medical checkpoints of age on pretty good terms. Yet it was just the other day that while in the leather chair in the living room, I sat at an odd angle for too long, and when I stood up, my back ached. It ached for two days straight. Just yesterday, my wife opened the medicine cabinet in the bathroom where I now stand and began to laugh. "Jesus," she said, "there's a lot of pills in here." True. One has a heart attack and high blood pressure, and one gets pills. Add painkillers for the dental work, and yes, there are "lots of pills in here."

The hat comes off and I move closer to the mirror. Without my glasses, I cannot see the detail of my upper front teeth and the gums that hold them, so I lean in tighter. Weathered teeth, teeth that have eaten tens of thousands of meals, held uncountable numbers of cigarettes when I was younger and cigars when I was older, teeth that have been soaked in 50 years of coffee and liquor. There's the one upfront with the tiny, nearly unnoticeable chip. The steel mouthpiece of my trombone collided with it during a marching-band routine in my junior year of high school. I haven't looked this closely at that chip in decades. The crowns will be set in the back upper right. A temporary filling hides the holes. Amazing how most of the teeth I see, nearly all of which have been with me for decades, have made it through the years—symbols of perseverance, badges of honor.

Two hours later, I'm heading home from the dentist, and can barely think of anything else but the single OxyContin in the pill bottle in the linen closet near the bathroom, a leftover from my wife's hip surgery a year ago. The pain is thumping. Breaking the rules, I will down the painkiller with a handful of water and think about a former student of mine who once wrote an essay about her debilitating high-school addiction to painkillers.

At home, I settle in to complete what I have been putting off over and over—my will. Since the first time I attempted this process, I have remarried, sold a house, moved several times, and consolidated money with my wife. Tomorrow, we travel to our accountant's office to work through tax returns, and so today, feeling confidently medicated, I settle in to finish minor items in the will, clarifying beneficiaries and who gets what—my parents' rings, father's drawings, and all that I have considered previously, but also something I recently rediscovered—a gold pocket watch my parents gave me as a high-school graduation gift. I found it in the back of a dresser drawer while looking for something else.

Working through this section of the online document is rather easy, and after completing it, I turn to the page on arrangements. Funeral? Burial? Memorial? Tradition? The program suggests a separate document, essentially a letter to those left behind. *These are my wishes*—the words one usually reads.

A traditional funeral is not for me; I don't want to be the dead man in a box surrounded by flowers as jacketed men and blushing women walk around the casket, kneeling before it, considering how stiff I look, how unlike me I am, touching my bloodless body and saying a meaningless prayer. What I want is a memorial. Talk about me, laugh at me, hug each other, drink beer, and make toasts with good Irish whiskey. Eat good food. Pray if you feel you need to, but pray for you, not me. Remember what I have left behind, salute it, and carry on. No burial. Cremation? That is an option. In Oregon there is what is called recomposition and it is legal. Your body is allowed to deteriorate and decompose into compost, soil and nutrients that can be used to nourish new life. I could be an evergreen on a mountain, or a wild geranium along a river. If it is legal when and where I die, I write in the will's addendum, this is my wish. If not, cremate me. Spread me where you wish. If you can make it happen, maybe some of the ashes near Dylan Thomas' boathouse in Wales, and along the shores of the English Channel on the Isle of Wight or off the coast of County Wexford. There is Jack Kerouac's home in Orlando. There is the desert of the American Southwest, where tossing dust into the red earth of the ancients seems more than fitting. Spread some near my old home in the steel town where I was born. *I know you will make the choices that are best and the most meaningful to you,* I write in the will's addendum. *Love, Your Father. Your Husband. Your Friend.*

Earlier in the day, when on the way home from the dentist, I heard the announcer on the radio conduct an interview with a medical professional about how the changing of the clocks scheduled for the coming weekend—the seasonal adjustment of time—might impact one's wellbeing. Daylight Saving Time returns, and so what began five months ago with the click of digits and the tunings of pointy clock hands is now returning to what had been. The length of a day's sunlight is being altered, again, giving us less illumination in the morning and more in the evening. It is the transference of time that is not unlike the act of growing old. If we are lucky, time is manipulated to favor what we cherish most, what gives us happiness or solace or contentment, while we take our pills, rub our aches, write the words others will read when we are dead, and try to keep the last of our teeth.

# 41

Puzzlement. Shadows are different, angles of sunlight sharper. Once it had been easy to judge the time of day by the light through the bedroom blinds. This is no longer the case. From my bed, the strength of the brightness of the morning is all around, more than I can remember from this position, the pillow propped under my head. It is new daylight with new minutes to count, one hour to be exact. The world has sprung forward.

There is an immediate need to know exactly what time it is, to know where I am in the universe of clocks, how to fit into the new morning daylight. I sit on the edge of the bed with my eyes on the window. What have I missed? What of the day is no longer? What can never be recovered? A bird tweets. A dog barks. The world is moving on. There is the old saying, an attribution linked to poets but none in particular: "Live by the sun and love by the moon." Native Americans believe the sun is the giver of life, the earth's guardian. And the moon offers serenity and protection. Live life, knowing something bigger than you is your guardian angel. Carl Sandburg wrote more than a half-dozen poems about the moon. Emily Dickinson may have penned more. She wrote, too, about the sun. So did Whitman, Plath, and Keats. George Harrison, too, gave us the sun. It goes on and on. My body and mind are tethered to that sun, yet the hands of society's clocks click off to the beat of history and world order. And at the same time, I am linked to the moon and its strange pull, knowing its fullness is coming. If it is a clear night, the moon will cast the shadows of tree-branches across the ground. The sun and the moon, the true measures of time— despite what the clocks say once they have all been reset, and despite how modern man lives in time's mercy.

# 42

The email came this morning.

Hello,

There is a vacancy at The Open Book from the 12th–18th April. We would like to offer this to you.

The message is from the bookstore in Wigtown along Scotland's southwest coast; the shop where I had been waitlisted; the shop where one can rent the upstairs apartment and run the place. The Bladnoch Distillery is a short distance away. There are mountains, rugged coast, moorland, and forest. It's quintessential Scotland. And it's waiting for me.

I hesitate, if only for a moment, to tell my wife. She is not Scottish, although she has some of the British Isles in her genes. She's never been and hasn't longed to visit England, Ireland, Scotland, or Wales like I have. She has never been as invested in this as I have been.

"Babe," I say, "Scotland is calling."

"The bookstore has an opening, doesn't it?"

Booksellers I know have told me that such an idea, at first, might appear to be a romantic undertaking. But running a bookstore is work, they have reminded me. Still, I wonder if some of the toil emanates from the burden of having a financial stake in the store as an owner, a manager, or one who relies on wages from the shop. The Open Book experience for me and my wife would have none of that kind of serious commitment. So, the romanticism could win over any unease or anxiety there might be.

"We can't go," my wife continues. "Your classes continue through May, right?"

"Not saying we would accept this one. But you do know what this means, don't you?"

"What?"

"This *is* going to happen. We have been given the opportunity. It's right there in front of us. Our names came up on the list. If we decline this time, which we'll have to, our names will remain. That's what the email says. And this means our time to run the shop *will* come. It *will* happen."

"Well, I guess I'm in," she says, smiling.

Someday it will happen. We will board a plane bound for Scotland, land in Glasgow, drive through the countryside, arrive in Wigtown on a sunny day, and be handed the keys to The Open Book. And we will unlock the store early and close it late, and we will drink hot tea at the counter and greet each patron, and talk about books, and suggest new works, and allow local poets to recite their verses aloud in the shop, and we'll make great new friends, and live the romantic bookseller life, even if it is just for a short time, even if it is in the middle of a notorious Scottish winter of rain and wind, even if after the first couple of days we realize it truly is what those seasoned booksellers had told us it is—hard work. Even then. Even then.

# 43

Donna is now floating at the bottom of the fishbowl. She appears to be dead, but when I tap the bowl with my finger, her fins flutter. It has been four days since she has last eaten. Weeks since she first showed signs of distress. Now, she barely moves.

"I think it's time to let her go," I say to my wife.

"Oh, I know, but I feel so bad about it."

"Think Oregon," I say.

Oregon, the state with assisted-suicide laws.

"But we don't know her wishes," my wife says. It's meant as a joke, but my wife means exactly what she says.

We've had the guppy for over two years since that unexpected purchase with my stepdaughter. Truth is, this is Donna-2. Donna-1 died in two days. But we still think of this one as simply Donna, the guppy that has now outlived her lifespan by nearly six months.

"I think we need to say goodbye," I say. "I won't flush poor Donna or bury her in the backyard unless my wife is okay with it."

Looking closer at the bowl, I tap the side again. Fins flutter, again.

Not long ago, our two dogs died here in this same kitchen where Donna now hangs on. Both dogs took their last breaths in my arms, one and then the other a year apart. Donna is not our dog, let's be honest. But there is life there, as fragile as it might be.

On the dining-room table, a few feet from Donna's bowl, are our newly completed last will-and-testaments, printed from the internet. The older ones, years out of date, are next to the new. The new ones need only the final signatures and a notary stamp. My wife has her beneficiaries clearly stated and so do I. There are contingencies and executors chosen. There is official legal language calling for no unusual means to keep us alive. And now together—my wife and I with the new documents, and an old fish—wait, each late in our collective lives, together and alone. The link of a dying guppy with our final wishes seems an odd thing, surely. The two together is only an accident, as everything is anyway.

# 44

It is good to be out on the bike again. Sunny and mild, the first ride in nearly a year. I'm a semi-regular seasonal cyclist, but riding today on the street with the traffic, as I have done so many times before, unnerves me. Regaining my ride-awareness will take some time. Each return takes more out of me. So, I move to the sidewalk, bumpy and uneven. Thank goodness for padded bike shorts. There is a breeze, and it makes the ride a chillier one, so I wear the shorts underneath long tight, black pants, the kind guys in yoga classes might wear. My body is not a yoga body, of which I am at this moment quite aware. I am also aware of how that body is working—my thighs, the blood rushing, and muscles burning.

Most of this stretch of the road is relatively flat, but there are at least two unavoidable ascents. The first is directly before me. I could shift gears, making the adjustment to give myself some assistance. Instead, for whatever reason, I plow forward, stay in gear, and wait to feel the firm tug of gravity. When it comes, I pedal harder. I burn. The cracked pavement is rough, forcing my wheels to wobble. I tighten my grip on the bars to retain balance. One minuscule distraction and I will go hard to the ground. One miscalculation is all it will take. An old fall flashes in my memory, a crash while crossing railroad tracks on this same route last summer on a rainy day, a tumble that slammed my helmeted head to the asphalt and bruised and bloodied my elbow and knee. For that split second, I had not been present; I had been anticipating my next turn and, lacking the nimbleness of youth, I lost control.

Ahead of me as I push forward, there is a woman. She is jogging, head down, running in the middle of the sidewalk. On one side is gravel, a bicyclist's must-avoid surface; and on the other, uneven dirt and dormant grass littered with small branches torn in winter from the nearby trees. After a moment of uneasiness, the woman looks up, waves, and takes her strides to the grassy side. "Thank you," I say in a husky breath. The woman nods. Despite earbuds, she has heard me. I trudge along, closing in on the top of the hill. Winded, I stop my pedaling. The bike glides on its own weight over the crest and downward. This is what the cyclist lives for, that exuberant downhill fall filled with wind and freedom. The old man is young again in that moment.

When the surface flattens, I return to pedaling. One tall tree of the many still bare is showing small green buds. There's a sign near the church for a coming father–daughter dance. A teenage boy in tattered jeans stands at the corner waiting for the bus, a ride, or a friend. I am no longer on the bike, it seems, not anymore, traveling now in another space. Annie Dillard wrote, "The present is an invisible electron." This is that present and I feel that pulse. It is an old feeling recovered from somewhere long ago, if only for an instant. Many times, it takes more work than I can muster to live in the present, to recognize that it is our memory in motion.

In 4 miles, I arrive at the half-point destination, the coffee shop in the town just west of my home.

"I know," I say to the clerk at the counter as I order a latte. "It must seem counterintuitive to drink coffee after a bike ride."

She giggles, glances at the helmet still on my head, and asks if that will be all.

I wonder what she's really thinking as I stumble using the app on my phone to pay for the coffee. It's not working well, or maybe I'm not working so well. Giving up, I pay with a credit card, and take the coffee in the far corner where I see my bike on the sidewalk rack near the door. *I did okay*, I think to myself. *It's been a long time, but I'm good. Four miles back home, no worries.*

Yes, I can do it, but can I jolt myself back to how I felt on the ride to where I am now? Can I sense again what Dillard called that "invisible electron"? I haven't lived my life in a state of *maybe tomorrow*, or *next time*. Sure, adventures have been delayed, desires postponed, longings shifted. Certainly, I have missed a million chances to be in the present, and maybe not faced the wind on that downhill ride as much as I should have.

As I click my helmet's strap and turn the bike away from the rack, I look east and then west. I look south. Which way to go? What route has more hills, more ups and downs, more chances to burn the muscles, to breathe hard, and then where will I rest and celebrate in the presence of an effortless breeze? Youth is only a state of mind, I tell myself. Somewhere just around the next bend in the road.

# 45

The sky above is like a blue blanket pulled over my head. It hangs low. There is a cooling, mild wind, but when it ceases for a moment, the sun warms. The dog and I plan to walk to our village downtown for a cup of coffee and to sit outside in the little square. It is exactly 1 mile. I feel I could walk much farther and longer. Solid sleep last night. Maybe it was the three tablets of melatonin before bed. Sustained sleep is not always easy for me. Falling into slumber comes quickly, but staying there is never consistent, not when restlessness arrives and, like an alarm, the bladder awakens me at 3 a.m. Last night, however, was different. The bathroom called, yes, but the usual restlessness was managed. And so now, I walk as if little in the world could stop me. It's remarkable to have this sensation, especially, dare I say, at my age. It doesn't come often enough anymore.

The dog and I move east along the rows of homes, past the park and the church, then south toward the train tracks. We wait for a few minutes at the gate for freight cars to rumble by. The dog is tied to a light pole outside the coffee shop, and I head inside to order. Across the street there is a stone bench under the trellis at the corner where we sit. The dog sniffs a discarded candy wrapper. It's a good spot. The sun is at my back. I am alive in the world. Then, for whatever reason, my mind shifts. *Is this what America calls retirement, is this what one does all day? Sitting on a bench in the sun? It is a wonderful afternoon, but this — every...single...day?* People everywhere do it all the time. Sit and ponder. Walk and watch. Old men sitting on benches drinking coffee.

"Let's go," I say to the dog as I rise. "I'm done here."

I walk west on the main street and think now of all that I have not been, never was, never will be. I'm in my sixties and I've never been to Tangier, never lived the life of a dangerous poet, as an expat in a bohemian village, a life like my literary heroes—Rimbaud, Burroughs, and Kerouac. Never lived the life of a troubled, starving, sentimentalized alcoholic, hashish-smoking artist, hanging out with other creatives in opium dens all night long. Never lived like an artistic recluse as Salinger did, or dedicated my life to nature and simplicity like Thoreau. Such romanticized dreams. These lives are never what they seem, of course. They are many times wretched. The truth is I never had the guts to find out what such a life might be, to experience any of it. Many years ago, I contemplated heading out on the road in a beat-up old van to play guitar and sing songs on any stage that would have me. Never did. Again, never had the guts to start the journey. I often think about this. But I always think again— does moving on this old dream take guts or is it recklessness? Is it a misplaced passion? Or is it regret? Maybe this state of mind, this way of thinking, is more madness than anything else. These other lives are not who I am, what I was, or ever have been. I'm a suburban white boy from a smoldering steel town, a boy from a working-class family whose father never finished high school and never could have imagined life as an artist, despite his incredible talent for creating pencil and charcoal drawings of dogs and birds and famous boxers. Bohemian lifestyle? Isolated artist? It took me until my early forties to understand what any of that meant. And here I am now, walking the dog in suburbia, passing a Domino's Pizza, holding a paper cup of dark roast from Starbucks, and wondering how in the world anyone arrives at this place in life with their soul intact.

At the railroad tracks, my cellphone buzzes. It's my son in Seattle.

"Hold on," I say. "Train passing. It's loud."

My son most certainly hears the heavy clanking, and the crossing-gate bells.

"Remind you of Illinois?" I ask once the train has rolled by.

"It does," he says.

The Chicago suburbs are train towns. Memories are built on aromas, they say, but sounds can evoke the same.

My son is calling to catch up. Checking in with Dad. We talk about work and our dogs, about his brother and his mother, his stepsister, what we had for dinner last night. Much of it is familiar. I talk as I cross the tracks, pass the library and the church, and take a seat on a park bench. *Old man on a bench drinking coffee.* We talk for a long time, and when it is time to say goodbye—still in my contemplative mood steeped in life's choices and ticking time—I wonder, what will it be like when my son can no longer call his father? When Dad doesn't answer? When I am unreachable? My sons and I talk, if not daily, four or five times a week. Short bursts of life to share. How will that be for them when I am gone?

"I love you," I say as I always do. He says the same, as he always does. And the call is over.

I don't believe I have regrets. But don't we all regret *something*? At least one thing? Sure, there is that artistic life I missed, the dangerous and the reclusive. But what if I had embraced that life in some way? What would that have done to my children? Would I have had children at all? I can't imagine a life like that. Not now. Not as I grow older and watch as my sons become men.

I walk slowly past the neighborhood houses toward home. The day is as it began, golden and embracing. Still no weariness in these old legs; my steps remain light. Yet the afternoon, the phone call, and those meandering thoughts have summoned weighty emotions. As the dog pulls toward a scampering squirrel on a fence, I consider what I should do with these unresolved sentiments about choices and children and life. It doesn't take much thought. I will do what Steinbeck did for his son, what Fitzgerald did for his daughter, what the fathers of Tim O'Brien and Jackson Pollock did for their sons.

I will write a letter.

# 46

The heavens fall toward me in graduating shades of blue. The trees are silhouettes in this early morning. It's quiet. I slept well. I am rested. And I walk to the shed, knowing what it is I want to say.

Dear boys,

I still call you boys. Funny, isn't it? Although you are grown men, leaning into your third decades in this world, you both will always be and always have been my boys. And here I am in the early light of a March day, considering my words, as I have done for so long. But this time, they come easily. I don't struggle for a hidden emotion or some imaginative spark. Instead, the words flow like the water in a mountain river after a long winter.

You can read this when you wish, but I've prepared myself to write it for you to read when I am gone, after you have said goodbye and memorialized me in some way, after you have scattered ashes or planted me somewhere, and after you have laughed at some silly moment with me, some dorky dad-ism, or cried with joy at a resurfaced memory of a trip we took together. Cuba comes to mind, when the three of us drank mojitos late at night in that small square in Havana and a street dog rested at our feet.

Why does a dad write to his sons? There are many reasons. I can tell you for certain that some of what I write here will be sappy. It's unavoidable. Some of it may also be sad. Maybe funny. Some advice, and some suggestions. All of it from deep inside. Some of it you have heard before, enough to roll your eyes. Some of it will surprise you. All of it, you must know, comes from a love so far beyond words.

Let's get grief out of the way.

It may be the most honest emotion of all when we allow it to be. But do not let grief keep you from laughing. That, too, is grief manifested. Both of you have senses of humor that permit the dark and absurd. Laugh. Please. Laugh at my death. Someone said once, in so many words, and I hope I'm not plagiarizing, but it goes something like this: It's not the rain that is painful. What's painful is trying to control the sun.

As I write, I think that maybe the best way to do this is to create a list. So, here goes.

Above all, express yourself. Express love to those you most care about. Friends. Family. Lovers. Don't let friendships fade. Time and space should not erode those dear connections. This seems simplistic and clichéd. But damn, it is not always easy to do.

Rebel. Question everything. Especially authority. Yes, I've told you this all your lives and maybe it has gotten you in trouble from time to time or put you in an uncomfortable or challenging place. But ultimately, you must question. And with this comes questioning yourself, too. Am I being the best I can be? Doing the right thing? Am I true to who I am and those I love? Am I kind?

Find someone to have coffee with, someone to break bread with, and someone to travel with. Being a human with humans will keep you alive.

Don't compare yourself to others. Screw others. You are you. Praise yourself. Be what you are. But be sure to take the time to find the real you. You can't be the best you without discovery. Take time to be alone, find passions, and open up to the world. Read. Sing songs. Do the things you are afraid to do.

Don't wait. Late is too late.

Be a Renaissance man. I already see this in the both of you, but don't ever stop adding to your talents. Cook new things, know how to drive a nail the right way, how to fix a sink, tie a tie, and dance a reasonable dance. Make music. Make a great Manhattan cocktail. Tell a good joke. Know the meaning of cultural references from film and literature. Memorize a poem.

Know when you are wrong. Say it out loud. Take responsibility. Own up. Avoiding this is weakness. Living this is powerful.

Hold no grudges. A grudge is a sign of weakness. Forgive. Always.

Be vulnerable. It leads to love and the most rewarding moments of your life.

Find time to walk and to live in nature.

Believe in something bigger than you.

Smile. It's infectious. Oh my, does that sound trite. But the simplest truths sometimes are the most profound.

I didn't always get it right, this fatherhood thing. Who truly knows what is right and wrong in the framework of this important job? I don't have regrets, but on some matters, do-overs would be nice. Still, if I were given that chance, I'm not sure I'd take the do-overs. There is an odd kind of beauty in the mistakes—giving up the ruse of Santa Claus too early, and those occasional mini-bursts of anger that seemed misplaced. The forgotten words at a wedding when I thought I had the officiating thing down pat. I did eventually get it right, though, didn't I? And when you were both in the early days of college, did I reach out enough? When I look back, I see it as a selfish time for me. Was I there for you? I hope so.

I think that's enough, enough to ponder or enough to make fun of, however you wish to digest these words. But before I stop, there is one last thought.

I have said so often how proud I am of my boys. But pride is a complicated emotion. Sometimes it is dreadfully selfish. I do not speak of pridefulness here, the idea that I should be acknowledged or praised for helping to create who you are. It is not about an ownership of the glory of what goodness you possess. Let me put it this way: I am not proud; I am impressed. I value you. I trust you. But mostly, I am impressed by who you have been, what you are now, and what you will become.

There are a hundred billion stars in the sky, my boys, and yours are the ones I see shining.

Love, Dad

## 47

It was a troubling dream, and it startled me awake. I don't remember all of it, but it had something to do with being lost in the woods. A maze of trees and no paths. The forest allowed for passageways through brush, yet none led to a clearing where I could see the village where I might be safe. The dream has unsettled me, my head now deep in the pillow, my eyes wide open. Then, in an instant, my mind pivots and I remember how I had forgotten to take my pills the night before. All those pills in the medicine cabinet. Neglecting to take any of them for one day, even several days, will not put me in jeopardy. Still, the pills, I'm told, are for the rest of my life. No matter how my heart continues to beat, no matter my blood pressure readings, no matter my weight or the plaque in my veins, no matter what the machines say, no matter the passing grades on the stress tests, I will for the remainder of my days stand at the cabinet in the bathroom, counting pills and downing them with a handful of tap water.

It is not quite dawn; a sliver of early light breaks through the bathroom window. I open the plastic pill bottles, and each click and snap is like a little bomb going off. The birds in the trees on the other side of the wall are deafening. The clank of a train in the distance sounds like thunder. Early morning is loud when you are trying to be quiet, trying not to awaken the house when you are considering what you do to keep going.

Tea in my cup, I sit in the leather chair next to a small lamp in the living room, and although I attempt to read, instead I count the beats of my heart. This must be what you do when you become keenly aware that the number of beats to come is fewer than those that have been. Forever counting beats, counting pills. We arrive in this world moving toward the light and then for decades we travel toward another light, the one that those who have come close to the end say they have witnessed—two lights, the one that leads us out of the womb and into the world, and the other commanding us somewhere eternal. All of us push against this reality, hoping to make the space between the lights as bright, and last as long, as one can. So, we take our pills. Walk our walks. Do our pushups. And we travel to New Mexico and worship the Earth God. Fly to Scotland to run a bookstore. Arrive in Ryde on the Isle of Wight and step along the beaches of my ancestors. Stand on a stretch of emerald earth before Black Rock Mountain in County Wexford. Between the two lights there is much to do. Like the daylight that shifts in the coldest season—the light that alternates the slant of the sun in our days—the space between birth light and death light is not forever. It has a beginning and an end. It is Standard Time and then it is not. And in the space between this, we are, in one way or another, fighting against the conclusion, hungering to capture a full existence, grab the good of life, if not simply trying for a string of good days, and moving head-on toward the task of growing older and carrying on.

# 48

The second cup of coffee this morning is the purer of the two. It was made on the stove, with a moka pot. The beans ground finely, espresso-style. The water boils through the coffee and bubbles out the stem into the pot. It is like witnessing the birth of something. The first cup was a latte, a double espresso with steamed milk. Although coffee has been made in a similar fashion—*café con leche, caffè e latte*—for decades in Italy, Spain, and France, the purest of coffee is made over a fire, a kind of boiling. The Italians certainly know how to produce a great coffee maker, but the coffee credit must go to a city in Yemen. The port town of Mokha is believed to be the first city to trade coffee. There is also the Ethiopian discovery story—an ancient herder, his goats, and local monks embracing the berries that would later be roasted. Certainly, some form of early moka pot had been developed, as coffee became a potential medicine in northern Africa and an aid in prayer for Muslims. So, with this, I drink my boiled coffee, black and thick and extraordinary.

When I was a young man, coffee came with sugar and milk. Somewhere in my forties, I dropped the sugar. In my fifties, I dropped the milk. Now, coffee at its richest is black, deep, and dark. Time changes us. Time changes taste. We are born with 9000 taste buds. By the age of 50, many are lost or have shrunk, experts say. And by 60, we may not be able to distinguish clearly between sweet, salty, and bitter. This sometimes means we lose our appetite. Tasting the coffee this morning is evidence that I have not yet lost my sense; the flavor of dark unsweetened chocolate and earth is on my tongue.

As a kid, I put ketchup on steak and grape jelly on my toast. I do neither now. Wouldn't dream of it. Lately, I have also found my intolerance for the heat made from spice fading away, adding hot peppers on my pizza, asking for medium hot dishes at the Thai restaurant, tossing a few more jalapeno slices in the nachos, and hot sauce on my eggs. The taste buds are shrinking, changing, and disappearing.

Age means change. Hair that was once shoulder length is now shaved closely. My waist is wider. I'm nearly an inch shorter than I was at the age of 30. But, of course, it is not only physical appearance that changes; so does our emotional self. The University of Edinburgh conducted a study that challenges everything we once thought about personality. Scientists followed a number of Scots from adolescence to old age—around 14 years old to 70. They conducted personality assessments along the way, measuring traits like self-confidence, perseverance, and mood stability. Strikingly, the younger and older selves appeared to show no resemblances. It was if the former youngster as an older person had been newly formed. Traditionally, it was believed that by the age of 30 or so, our personalities were set in stone. Maybe that is simply not true. The only constant—even when it comes to the essence of who we are and what we become, our beliefs, our loves, and desires—is change.

The coffee of my youth is not the coffee of my todays, a metaphor for the time gone by, you might say. Time has molded and sculpted a new me, and now here I am, at the kitchen counter, sipping what I would have never imagined tasting as a 15-year-old boy experiencing the first cup of sweet and milky American brew my grandmother had made to match my youthful taste buds. Here I am aging; growing older with wrinkles around the eyes, gray hairs on my chin, transformed and evolved. I do not wish youth to return, and I do not fear this journey of growing old. Susan Sontag said doing such a thing would be "abusing the present." I would not wish to do that. So, I drink. The coffee is too good.

# 49

On a short walk after lunch a few days following the official time change, I notice an old dog. *Why haven't I noticed him before?* He sits near the edge of a long driveway, paws outstretched. Gray hair surrounds his snout and at the tips of his ears, encroaching on the black at the top of his head, neck, and shoulders. He is attentive, examining me as I pass, but it is only his head that moves as I do, his watery eyes on mine. No longer does he care to bark, have the need or the desire to alert the world to my presence. He must remember younger days when he would stand alert and snap at the walking man; he recalls when it was his duty and his purpose. But now, satisfied with his place in time, he watches without concern. Calm to the world. Content.

W. B. Yeats wrote that in aging, we lose "something of the lightness of our dreams." Maybe the act of growing older—for dog or man—is simply a transformation of energy, a shift, a mystical change in perception because no one really understands time anyway.

Heading home, I promise myself to print the letter I've written to my sons, seal it in an envelope, and place it in a folder along with my will.

# 50

It has been two weeks since the time change, but today it is officially spring, the season's first full day. It comes earlier in the calendar this year, this eternal marker for new beginnings, new promise—so here I am, heading out in its earliest hours to a forest of ponds, prairie, and maples.

A long, winding road to St. James Farm leads my dog and me past open fields, tall trees, and grasses toward a decades-old complex. Working stables had once been part of this preserve, the one-time estate of the McCormick family, a wealthy and influential clan. They raised horses and dairy cows. It is a sprawling, stately place, donated by the family for all others to experience. Wedding receptions are held here now. There are two cars in the parking lot near the edge of a trail that leads north toward strands of trees. I'm carrying a cigar. My mood calls for it, a kind of quiet celebration. But not wanting to present the musty, earthy aromas of burning tobacco to others who are trying to find a bit of peace in the forest, I take the grassy path to the west, instead. It is less traveled.

The ground is mushy. Brown dormant grasses are underfoot. But the air is fresh and sweet. The trees are without early buds here, but as Chekhov wrote when recalling the trees of spring, "they are already living and breathing." We take a slight hill toward a pond of still, dark water. In the center is a wooden bird feeder. Canada ducks swim around it. As a kid coming upon water like this in the Pennsylvania forest, there would be tall pussy willows lining the banks. My friends and I would pull them from the ground to bring home and Mom would place them in a glass vase. My mother always said that pussy willows, more than any other wild plant, reminded her of early spring.

She was not schooled in nature, but she was awed by it, never missing an autumn trip to the mountains to see the changing leaves. She took great care in her garden, especially with her lilies of the valley, finding joy in watching them rise out of the dirt in the first days of the season. No flowering plants in the preserve here today, but under one tree I spot the green leaves of early tulips, spring unfolding.

On the other side of the pond, some 75 yards away, is a magnificent tree. It sits alone, no others or plants nearby. The trunk is broad and husky, and the bark is as craggy as the face of a North Atlantic fisherman. The canopy is massive. It is a weeping willow. Not uncommon, certainly, yet when there are no buds or leaves, it is more difficult to identify. I run my fingers across the deep crevices in the bark, stand next to the trunk, and look up through the twists and turns of its gray-brown branches. There is an abundance of power. For centuries the weeping willow was associated with the tears of those who had lost loved ones, its drooping branches laden with sorrow. But the tree is also one of the most flexible, one of the few that can bend without breaking. It is a fast grower and can thrive in harsh winters and dry hot summers and can easily be reproduced by simply placing a twig in moist earth. Grief is not all the willow lives for. Monet painted a series of willows in response to the tragedy of World War I, but his shadowy forms not only evoke sadness toward war, but also arouse a kind of melancholy and longing best suited to a poet. Is this grief or strength? It all depends on the light and the season.

At the top of another hill is an odd contraption. It's a cylinder about a foot tall attached to the top of a skinny wooden stand stuck in the ground. Below the square roof that hangs over the cylinder is a small oblong hole, about 3 inches in diameter. Underneath are words stenciled in black:

## BLUEBIRD NESTBOX
## TAMPERING VIOLATES FEDERAL LAW

The bluebird is the symbol of goodness and joy. The bluebird of happiness. The bird Native Americans believe is the sign of spring, the bird with the song that is meant to drive your troubled and hard times away, the bird sometimes seen as a guardian angel with a message. I look closely at the hole. There is nothing inside the nestbox. Behind me and in the distance, there is no evidence of the bluebird, yet in the breeze I hear an undistinguishable chirp. Wouldn't it be nice if it were the bluebird's song? Its message would come on its wings—good things to come, many days in your future, health, and gladness.

The dog and I climb farther up the hill to the twist in the trail. The cigar takes effort to light in the breeze, but it finally catches. Over the pond and across the field is a cluster of old trees, stark limbs everywhere, all of this left behind by the exiting winter. There is little sound now, only that of a breeze on the branches. Time stills. The cigar assists the mood. Introspection comes easier with a cigar. Smoking one slows the mind. You simply cannot smoke a cigar quickly. It requires one to take time, to settle in, to look harder, to listen, to see more. Smoking a cigar is not my usual routine, but when I do, as in this moment, it demands a quieter rhythm. It is the men of a certain age who understand the meditative nature of a cigar. The young try too hard; they rush the burn. The old know a cigar's purpose. They understand.

The trail moves up to the crest of the hill and through a strand of old-growth trees. It snakes to a clearing and bends back around toward the complex. Emerging from a gathering of oaks, I see a lone tree to the west in a small valley. One of its large low-hanging limbs has been cut away. It is a fresh cut. One can see this clearly from the tan and caramel browns of the inner wood and the surrounding heartwood. From my view, this cut in the tree, where a hefty branch had once stretched out from the trunk, appears to form a natural portrait of the Healer's Hand, the ancient spiral design inside the palm. It is easy to see. No searching required, no standing at a particular angle of light. The visual is without question. The colors and shades—the fingers, the hand's center, the shadows in the wood's colors—are as if they had been sketched on the cut-away wood, a prehistoric symbol of eternity, the deity of the Spirit.

After following the trail for another half-mile, the cigar has burned to a stubby butt, too short to stay lit. I stamp it against the sole of my boot to be sure it is out and tuck it in my coat's pocket to be tossed away later. The dog's stride has slowed. She is tiring. We have had our walk, our woodland retreat, and we are ready to head home. But for a moment, I hesitate. I believe I could walk forever, moving across the field and into the dense trees to the south, stepping off toward nothing, no destination, no point of victory or finish. This is conviction and my hope. Maybe someday I will walk the West Highland Way in Scotland, the Camino de Santiago in Spain, the Pine Tree Trail in New Mexico, and the coastal footpath on the Isle of Wight. Maybe it will be early springtime, like now when daylight is lengthening, when the world is reawakening. Maybe I will be strong enough to travel one more mile, to climb one more hill, to cross one more creek. Maybe this will be time's gift. Maybe when I recall the many walks—the ones abandoned, and the ones never imagined—maybe then, and only then, will I say that I have done what I set out to do. Maybe then, and only then, might I confess to what has and has not been, and be content with it, satisfied in what is and what never was, and what has been left by the side of the long, bending path. I think of this now as I exit this gentle land in the low light of day, on this first spring day, at a time when the trail's end is closer than where it began.

# About the Author

David W. Berner has written several books of personal narrative and fiction, including the award-winning novel *A Well-Respected Man* and the memoir *Any Road Will Take You There*. He has received honors from The Society of Midland Authors, the Chicago Writers Association, the Eric Hoffer Awards, and has served as the Writer-in-Residence at the Jack Kerouac Project in Orlando, Florida, and at the Hemingway Birthplace Home and Museum in Oak Park, Illinois. David is also a journalist, broadcaster, and former associate professor at Columbia College Chicago.

# Notes

These artists and their works have helped to inspire and elevate this book.

Dylan Thomas, "The Force That Through the Green Fuse Drives the Flower"

W. H. Auden, "As I Walked Out One Evening"

W. B. Yeats, "When You Are Old"

Robert Frost, "Dust of Snow"

Neil Young, "Old Man"

John Lennon and Paul McCartney, "In My Life"

David Crosby, "By the Light of Common Day"

George Orwell, *Down and Out in Paris and London*

Pablo Picasso, *Old Guitarist*

Georges Seurat, *A Sunday Afternoon on the Island of La Grande Jatte*

Andy Warhol, *Camouflage*

Jim Harrison, "Walking"

Jack Kerouac, *The Dharma Bums*

Allen Ginsberg, *Wait Till I'm Dead*

Ernest Hemingway, *A Moveable Feast*

Carl Sandburg, "Under the Harvest Moon"

Emily Dickinson, "I Watched the Moon Around the House"

# O-BOOKS

# SPIRITUALITY

O is a symbol of the world, of oneness and unity; this eye represents knowledge and insight. We publish titles on general spirituality and living a spiritual life. We aim to inform and help you on your own journey in this life.
If you have enjoyed this book, why not tell other readers by posting a review on your preferred book site?

**Recent bestsellers from O-Books are:**

### Heart of Tantric Sex
Diana Richardson
Revealing Eastern secrets of deep love and intimacy
to Western couples.
Paperback: 978-1-90381-637-0 ebook: 978-1-84694-637-0

### Crystal Prescriptions
The A–Z guide to over 1,200 symptoms and their healing crystals
Judy Hall
The first in the popular series of eight books, this handy little guide is packed as tight as a pill bottle with crystal remedies for ailments.
Paperback: 978-1-90504-740-6 ebook: 978-1-84694-629-5

## Shine On

David Ditchfield and J S Jones

What if the aftereffects of a near-death experience were undeniable? What if a person could suddenly produce high-quality paintings of the afterlife, or if they acquired the ability to compose classical symphonies? Meet: David Ditchfield.

Paperback: 978-1-78904-365-5 ebook: 978-1-78904-366-2

## The Way of Reiki

The Inner Teachings of Mikao Usui

Frans Stiene

The roadmap for deepening your understanding of the system of Reiki and rediscovering your True Self.

Paperback: 978-1-78535-665-0 ebook: 978-1-78535-744-2

## You Are Not Your Thoughts

Frances Trussell

The journey to a mindful way of being, for those who want to truly know the power of mindfulness.

Paperback: 978-1-78535-816-6 ebook: 978-1-78535-817-3

## The Mysteries of the Twelfth Astrological House

Fallen Angels

Carmen Turner-Schott, MSW, LISW

Everyone wants to know more about the most misunderstood house in astrology — the twelfth astrological house.

Paperback: 978-1-78099-343-0 ebook: 978-1-78099-344-7

## WhatsApps from Heaven
Louise Hamlin
An account of a bereavement and the extraordinary
signs — including WhatsApps — that a retired
law lecturer received from her deceased husband.
Paperback: 978-1-78904-947-3 ebook: 978-1-78904-948-0


## The Holistic Guide to Your Health
## & Wellbeing Today
Oliver Rolfe
A holistic guide to improving your complete health,
both inside and out.
Paperback: 978-1-78535-392-5 ebook: 978-1-78535-393-2


## Cool Sex
Diana Richardson and Wendy Doeleman
For deeply satisfying sex, the real secret is to reduce the heat,
to cool down. Discover the empowerment and fulfilment
of sex with loving mindfulness.
Paperback: 978-1-78904-351-8 ebook: 978-1-78904-352-5


## Creating Real Happiness A to Z
Stephani Grace
*Creating Real Happiness A to Z* will help you understand
the truth that you are not your ego
(conditioned self).
Paperback: 978-1-78904-951-0 ebook: 978-1-78904-952-7

## A Colourful Dose of Optimism

Jules Standish

It's time for us to look on the bright side, by boosting
our mood and lifting our spirit, both in our interiors,
as well as in our closet.

Paperback: 978-1-78904-927-5 ebook: 978-1-78904-928-2

Readers of ebooks can buy or view any of these bestsellers by
clicking on the live link in the title. Most titles are published
in paperback and as an ebook. Paperbacks are available in
traditional bookshops. Both print and ebook formats are
available online.

Find more titles and sign up to our readers' newsletter at
**www.o-books.com**

Follow O books on Facebook at **O-books**

For video content, author interviews and more, please subscribe to our YouTube channel:

## O-BOOKS Presents

Follow us on social media for book news, promotions and more:

## Facebook: O-Books

## Instagram: @o_books_mbs

## Twitter: @obooks

## Tik Tok: @ObooksMBS

www.o-books.com